Path of Shadows, Flickering Light

Path of Shadows, Flickering Light

Living Toward Death as a Christian Pastor

CORDELL STRUG

RESOURCE *Publications* · Eugene, Oregon

PATH OF SHADOWS, FLICKERING LIGHT
Living Toward Death as a Christian Pastor

Copyright © 2021 Cordell Strug. All rights reserved. Except for brief quotations in critical publications or reviews, no part of this book may be reproduced in any manner without prior written permission from the publisher. Write: Permissions, Wipf and Stock Publishers, 199 W. 8th Ave., Suite 3, Eugene, OR 97401.

This is a work of non-fiction, but of memory, not research, and some names and details have been changed to mask identities.

Scripture quotations are from the New Revised Standard Version Bible, Copyright © 1989 National Council of the Churches of Christ in the United States of America. Used by permission. All rights reserved worldwide.

Resource Publications
An Imprint of Wipf and Stock Publishers
199 W. 8th Ave., Suite 3
Eugene, OR 97401

www.wipfandstock.com

PAPERBACK ISBN: 978-1-7252-9611-4
HARDCOVER ISBN: 978-1-7252-9612-1
EBOOK ISBN: 978-1-7252-9613-8

03/02/21

For all the dying

...all stories, if continued far enough, end in death, and he is no true-story teller who would keep that from you.

—Hemingway, *Death in the Afternoon*

Then the telephone becomes a tinkling terror, because it tells you of the sudden deaths of men and women that you knew intimately...

—Kipling, *The Man Who Would Be King*

Arise, cry out in the night,
>   at the beginning of the watches!
Pour out your heart like water
>   before the presence of the Lord!
Lift your hands to him
>   for the lives of your children...

—Lamentations 2:19

Set your minds on things that are above, not on things that are on earth, for you have died, and your life is hidden with Christ in God.

—Colossians 3:2–3

CONTENTS

Acknowledgments	ix

Introduction: Living and Dying Creatures

I	xiii
II	xv
III	xix

Part One: Bodies and Rites: Learning

I	3
II	6
III	8
IV	10
V	13
VI	15

Part Two: Bodies and Rites: Serving

I	23
II	26
III	28
IV	32
V	37
VI	40
VII	42
VIII	46
IX	50
X	53
XI	55
XII	58
XIII	59
XIV	62

Part Three: For All the Saints

I	65
II. Kay	66
III. Caitlyn	70
IV. Loyal	74
V. Raymond	79
VI. James	82
VII. Wayne	86
VIII	89

Part Four: Without Form and Void

I	95
II	99
III	103
IV	108
V	113
VI	117

Brief Epilogue in Time of Plague

ACKNOWLEDGMENTS

Several people deserve thanks for agreeing to look at parts of this writing: Amanda Bergstrom, Paul Cannon, Cathy Daharsh, Peter Geisendorfer-Lindgren, Gary and Ruth Halverson, Ron and Pat Henning, Rick Hest, Mary Preus, Paul Sponheim, and Mary Carol Strug.

Paul Cannon, Peter Geisendorfer-Lindgren, Gary Halverson, and Paul Sponheim shared their thoughts on ministry and assured me that pastors young and old struggle with the same things I did. Gary Halverson and Paul Sponheim suggested I add some thoughts on life during the coronavirus outbreak. Mary Preus, with detailed commentary, made the book much clearer than it might have been. Most of my readers have shared with me, through the years, their adventures in aging. I must thank as well the gracious and efficient staff at Wipf and Stock, especially my project manager, Matt Wimer, who coped patiently with all my nervous e-mails. Finally, Sylvia Ruud, my partner in literary adventures, was the crucial figure in this project. She urged me to take it on and, when it was floundering, clarified its nature and helped give it its final shape.

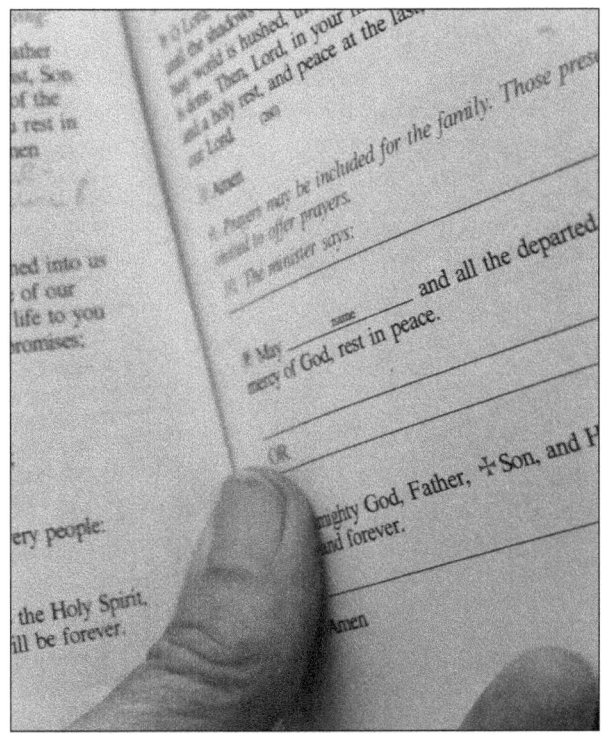

INTRODUCTION

Living and Dying Creatures

I

A great part of my working life and, thus, a great part of my life was spent thinking about and talking about death. My spouse Mary Carol and I served as pastors in the Lutheran church (LCA, then ELCA) and, for reasons not important here, we served our time together, as co-pastors, mostly in two small rural Minnesota parishes. It was the nature of those parishes that brought death close as a daily reality. The first was in the Northwest corner of the state, about twenty miles from Canada and twenty miles from North Dakota. At the time, with most of the farms gone and most of the population elderly, our county had the highest death rate in the state. In one three-week period, when we were supposed to be on vacation, we had five funerals. After almost sixteen years, when we were interviewing at the second parish we would serve, a member of the call committee assured us they really didn't have that many funerals. But in our first year we were planning and presiding at one every other week.

Serving those communities for so long, it was impossible to ignore or hide from the realities of aging and dying. Emergency rooms, hospital stays, lives adjusting to the failures of bodies, funerals, and grieving were fundamental, sometimes overwhelming, parts of our life together. The presence and the pressure of death in life was undeniable, a steady beat under all our doings.

I subtitled this work: living toward death as a Christian pastor. I intended that as a layered characterization. All of us are living toward death, whether we know it or not, accept it or not; it's the knowledge we have to gain, the acceptance we grant or deny. For Christians, death is part of our lifelong meditation: our foundational story, our prayers, and our songs. Christians don't necessarily accept the reality of death any more readily than anyone else; but there's a place prepared for it in the story we tell about life. Pastors carry in them both the creature's mortality and the Christian story, but their life toward death has its own intensity, its own shape, its own awareness.

It's given to pastors to wrestle with the deaths of others. Pastors are some of the prime actors in a community's grappling with death and finding its way back to life. The life of a pastor, in ministries where funerals are frequent, narrows again and again to an all-consuming involvement in attending a death, planning and presiding at a funeral, and creating a sermon to sum up one life, one loss, our grief, our hope, and all our fragile living.

Now that I've been retired a bit and have lived beyond my three-score years and ten, I sense the nearness of death in a more immediate way but I sense it after a lifetime of meditating on its force and nature. I wouldn't say we're approaching each other as old friends, but we've hung around in the same neighborhoods and we've certainly bumped into each other a lot.

So I wanted to reach back and trace the shadow of death as it fell across my life: in Part One, how it first touched me and showed me its force; in Part Two, how it expanded and darkened, and how I wrestled with it in my calling; in Part Three, how I spoke for my congregations in its presence; in Part Four, how it looks to me now as I await it. (As the novel coronavirus came upon us shortly after I finished this writing, I've added a brief epilogue with some thoughts on life during the outbreak.) But first, because death is always the death of someone, I want to speak of one particular death.

II

This is a scene that remains with me vividly from my service, one that rises up from memory whenever my thoughts turn to mortality. It seems to have a significance for me I'm not sure I can express completely, but I want to begin with it because it was a wordless scene. I think it's important to remember, especially in such a word-filled tradition as the one I served in, that much of our response to death is beyond and beneath language, in all the mysteries of our silence, our ignorant brooding, our senseless presence. We respond most naturally and most deeply to death with something like its own impenetrable silence.

Here is what comes back to me:

I'm sitting at the bedside of a very old woman whom I've known for years, and I'm listening to her breathe. Her name is Kay, I like her a lot, she's over a hundred years old, and no one thinks she can live through the night. We're alone, in the near dark, only one dim light on in her small room in the quiet care center where most everyone is asleep. I've said the prayers I usually say with those nearing death and now I'm sitting with my hand on hers, my prayer book in my lap, and all I can hear is her breathing. It sounds like she has to rip the air she needs from what surrounds her. It's the sound of life, of the spirit, desperate now, almost finished with the flesh.

Some strange thoughts haunted me as I sat there, but here I want to hold up the purity of the scene itself. We were two creatures of earth, together in the dark, one dying, one watching. Everything else is put into the shadows by that truth. It seems to me something as natural to us as eating or sleeping, as touching or clinging. It seems deeper than any system of belief: one living creature being present and watching over one dying creature. It seems the very seed of all ceremonies of farewell.

It's an act at the limit of our powers: the falling toward absence of the dying leaves us little to do at their bedsides but be there. It purifies the being there.

I sometimes think it odd that it's Kay's death, not any of the deaths in my family, that comes to me first as an image of dying. But pastors are privileged to attend the deaths of others, to be with the families of others in the most agonizing and unguardedly painful scenes, and those are the deaths that remained most real to me. I've wondered if this says something about me alone, that my calling was the most engaging part of my living; but I've wondered, too, if being present *as a pastor* wasn't a way of diluting the force of death, masking its ugly irrationality. The deaths of others came to me, from the start, as more than a loss: they came to me as part of my mission, a call to bring something to them. My calling gave them a meaning, a moral dimension. I think we'd do almost anything to run from and hide from the emptiness of death, the dark absence that shuts us out completely.

Or maybe everything about our lives makes less sense than we like to think.

Kay and I were only together in her last moments because of the brute reality of happenstance, the random crossing of paths which give us the people we meet, live with, and die beside. Kay's congregation was the second that Mary Carol and I served and we'd been called to it a few years before this night. Kay was already in the care center when we came, quite frail but always cheerful. She was one of my favorite stops when I was out visiting.

Her family had been part of the church for a long time. She had two sisters still living, also quite elderly, who had married two brothers because their farms were close and they shared a car. The husbands were gone and the sisters now lived together. They came to worship every week, but they no longer drove at night. So they asked us, as Kay's end seemed near, if we could go and sit with her, if the end should come at night.

They didn't want to think of her dying alone. It was, again, that need for presence, the vigil at the passing, that needs no explaining. Of course, we agreed.

They left our number at the care center and, one night as we were going to bed, the call came. It's always hard to tell over the phone how serious something is, and nurses react at different speeds, but I didn't mind driving out and would have hated letting the family down, so off I went.

This was a good care center. The night nurse cared enough to keep close watch and to make the call. It always smelled clean, and the first thing you notice about the bad ones is they don't. There were always a lot of aides around, lots of cheerful talk, and there weren't distressed patients struggling alone in their wheelchairs. In other words, this was a privileged and a peaceful death. This really was a place of care. There are much worse places and much worse ways to die.

Most of the deaths I was present at or involved with were peaceful. Our little towns had their share of deaths by accident, and my wife preached at the funerals of both a murdered father and a murdered mother. The troubled child who did the killing in each case sat in the pews during the service. But, by and large, those we served escaped most of the things we pray to be delivered from in the Great Litany: war, bloodshed, and violence, epidemic, drought, and famine, earthquake, fire, and flood.

Kay was dying the death we would all have to die, even if we were lucky enough to escape all the world's horrors, even if we could afford every balm and every comfort. When I entered her room, she had already fallen into herself, she was beyond noticing me, and her living was only a gasping for air.

I would have said, as I sat there, that I knew very well that I would die, because I knew all of us would die. Yet looking back, I think I still helplessly perceived death as an intrusion, something that happened to others. I would have told you that, after years of church service, years of funerals, watching the leadership of congregations age and pass on their tasks, I was well aware of the way generations shift, how they touch, bond, and part in overlapping days. But I think I would have spoken as a detached observer, not as someone aware of how short his own span of days might be.

It wasn't all that strange sitting next to Kay while she was oblivious to me. I had done that a lot. Over the years, she increasingly repeated herself and the loop of her conversation grew shorter and shorter. She always dismissed me with great courtesy when she became too tired to continue, thanking me for visiting. If she nodded off, I would sit there a bit anyway and, lately, more and more of her time was spent in sleep.

It wasn't strange either to sit listening to someone gasping for breath. I had done that a lot, too. I was called one night around midnight, followed an ambulance to the hospital, and sat with a woman until dawn as we wondered how her husband managed to keep breathing. Then, at dawn, his breathing cleared, and eventually he went home, for a time.

But when the breathing does stop, it's the strangest and simplest thing. It just stops. Maybe more accurately: one gasp follows another and another until one doesn't. It's as though you've been walking with someone and suddenly realize they've turned aside and you've left them behind: you realize you're no longer hearing the only thing you were listening to.

I sat with Kay for about half an hour. Then she was still. I noted the time so I could tell the nurse at the desk. I traced a cross on Kay's forehead and said a prayer of commendation.

But here's the oddest thing I remember: it felt odd getting up to leave the room. Just walking out without saying anything more, or more personal—or: with no one to say anything to—seemed almost rude, as though I were turning my back on someone I should be helping, or it seemed weirdly detached, as though life had skipped a track or shifted into another dimension, some parallel world that Kay wasn't in. I think it was the sudden absence: there was no way to assimilate it or find a place for it. Kay died a natural death, but death itself, as expected as it was, suddenly seemed unnatural, out of place, not part of our place.

Again, though, the hard truth prevails: it didn't matter how I felt. I had to walk out and set the next tasks in motion: the care center would have to send Kay's body on to the funeral home; someone unknown to me would have to tidy up finances, possessions, legacies; my spouse and I would begin preparing the service and the church arrangements; all who knew Kay would begin their grieving, remembering, healing, forgetting. All this brings, I guess, the only order we can offer, the way we make a place for death.

If I look back now and see myself walking down the darkened hall to the nurses' desk, I see a healthy, confident professional. I don't think I appreciated how effortlessly alert and awake I was that late at night, how well I saw the road when I drove there, how I could stand up without my right knee wobbling or stabbing me with pain, how I walked without stiffness, how I had travelled, sat so long, and returned home without once looking for a restroom. I don't think I could have imagined that a time might come for me when the way Kay slept away the days would seem a sensible and attractive way to live.

III

If I died today, I would have lived one of those lives that give pastors an easy time in their funeral sermons: I did live my three score and ten; most of my health problems have been broken bones from stupid accidents; I'm healthy enough to run with my dog and mostly avoid my doctors; I've been married for over fifty years; I've been able to find ways to use whatever talents I was given; I've seen my children grow and, before the coronavirus pandemic, I ate lunch with one of my grandchildren every other week. I'm sure some dutiful and good-hearted pastor will check these off on the scorecard of my blessings and consolations, just as I once did.

Even the injustices of birth tilted my way: born a white male in the United States in the middle of the twentieth century, I had opportunities and resources before me that most people of the earth, living and dead, were never offered. An African-American child growing up a few blocks away from me in Chicago would have had few of them.

I know the ancient caution: count no one happy until death. Still, as my Scandinavian parishioners would say: my life could have been worse. It really could have been.

I was tempted, when I began this introduction, to say something like: my calling gave me more reason than most people have to be aware of death in life. But that would have been, at best, silly and, at worst, obscenely blind to the horrors and the violence, the diseases and the torments, the very shortness of life that most people of other times and other places were never, and are never, able to ignore. As an added twist to my privilege, there are places as I write where people have been being killed and mutilated by the thousands for years in the careless wars waged by the same nation that is coddling me as one of its senior citizens.

I might say: living toward death as a Christian means knowing and admitting the marks of sin that bring suffering and death to the world I'm living my privileged life in, and that privileges like mine are some of those marks. But then, Christians have traditionally seen death itself as the deepest mark of sin, the one that takes us to our corruption, the one no creature, however privileged, can escape.

Now I want to go back to my beginnings, when death and I first began to meet.

PART ONE

Bodies and Rites: Learning

I

My first memories of death are also memories of funerals. I grew up in a Polish Roman Catholic community on the South Side of Chicago, a parish so large it had four Masses every morning and six on Sundays. There would usually be two and sometimes as many as six acolytes (or "altar boys," as we were known then) serving at each Mass, but this was the post-war baby boom era and the parochial school I attended had forty or fifty students in each class. I can't remember now if it was by being chosen or by volunteering, but I was often called out of class during the week to be one of the acolytes serving at a funeral Mass.

These were the days before white vestments and songs of victory brought the proclamation of new life, days when death was confronted as the price of sin and the stark reminder of inevitable loss and failure, the more than likely consignment to punishment, now too late to avoid. Unless my memory is faulty, our vestments were black and, with the still formal and distant service, the mysterious Latin words, the enforced and eerie silence of the chancel's sacred space, it was a sober, solemn experience. The priests were the same priests we all had to tell our sins to in confession, so they presided as our judges, our disciplinarians. At the funeral, the presence of the body in the coffin brought its own silence and strangeness. There was incense, too, and for Roman Catholics, the vision of purgatory as the next stage of the human journey, promising its own measure of purifying misery. (I remember, much later in life, having freed myself of much of this, being struck at my mother's funeral by the sense that, in the eyes of the church, she was almost beginning a second life.)

This really was a severe and affective ordering of death. In other words, death came to me first wrapped up in ritual, put into order by ritual, a ritual shaped to its reality but resembling our common Mass enough to be familiar. Death appeared not as an irrational threat, but with its meaning and purpose provided. I couldn't have known I would spend quite a bit of my life presiding and preaching at funerals, but I knew very early the power of ritual to meet death and strengthen the grieving.

And yet my knowledge of that power was qualified by my youthful ignorance of the power and the spiritual force of death itself, my ignorance of loss and grief.

In fact, when I think of leaving class to serve at those masses, I see myself leaving with a swagger, feeling specially chosen and very superior to those I was leaving in their seats, enslaved to the lessons and the clock. I felt the funeral as a liberation. Since school, at that time, meant sitting for hours at the same desk, mostly in grimly enforced silence, the sense of freedom in leaving class for any reason hardly needs explaining. Still, beyond my shallow enjoyment, associating death with liberation has become one natural way we have of coming to terms with it.

When I first studied Platonism, I found the idea of the soul being freed from the prison of the body as both a description of death and a way of living toward death so obviously true, not to mention desirable, I wondered how anyone could question it. No doubt a religious upbringing disposes many of us to be attracted to Platonic philosophy. (Being an overweight teenager, suffering daily the body's grossness, probably helped, too.) But it has struck me that some of the force of my attraction to this philosophy may have come from my early experience of death's coming as a time of freedom.

Then, too, a funeral really is as much a departure from ordinary time as a festival is, a calling out from the mundane to time and activity that is set apart, literally out of the ordinary, special time. There's the same escape from business and drudgery, the same elevation of fundamental realities and the revelation of value, the same fading of the future's clutter before the irresistible demands of the day at hand. If burying someone is, literally and grimly, saying farewell to the flesh, it is also a carnival in the common and festive sense.

People really do enjoy themselves at funerals: they enjoy being together, they enjoy reconnecting with friends and family, they enjoy telling stories and reviving memories of the dead, all the dead. They enjoy laughing and bringing back to life the fun and the goodness of life they remember.

But that's not all they do, not all they feel. And I did get a glimpse, at those services, of the darker side of the reality I was a small and ignorant part of, something beyond my free time, something beyond ritual, all the fear and misery we gather our weapons against.

It was right at the end of the service and it's the single moment of that time that comes back to me most powerfully.

This was a congregation of Poles, many of them born in Poland, some of them, like my grandmother, still barely able to speak English, and the old ways were still strong. So, at the end of the Mass, after all the prayers, blessings, and ritual gestures were done, we processed down the aisle, leading the coffin, followed by the family. In my church, it was a long aisle. But we didn't process all the way out: we stopped near the end and turned round to face the mourners while the choir went into a wailing, almost howling, Polish lament. After the Latin of the service, the Polish words came as a plunge down into earthy, messy, vulgar life.

And I can still remember the shock I felt as I turned with the priest to face the survivors, in my happy morning freedom, held tightly by the funeral rite. It was an almost physical shock, like being slapped. I'm at the priest's left, I seem to not be very tall, I'm about the length of the coffin from the first row of the family, and I see people twisted into misery, faces distorted and bodies sagging, quivering, and leaning into each other, clutching each other, shrieking sobs like a hellish descant over the choir's lament. It was a grief beyond anything I was able to grasp. It was outside the normal in a wilder, more threatening way. It was like watching people hit by a sudden, powerful storm. I felt ashamed in my watching, as though I had no right to witness such naked suffering.

It was the one moment that I began to glimpse something of what death's coming brings.

II

And yet I might have taken that knowledge from the Christian faith itself. At the heart of its life, in its worship, its meditations, its prayers and its art, its visions and its demands, there is death: not just the idea of death, not even the natural human death my parishioner Kay died, but a horrible death: a tortured, broken man, an outcast deliberately executed, abandoned and slowly dying, denied all the ceremonies we've invented to veil the reality. Christians worship through the image of a torn and mutilated body, a pierced sack of flesh leaking the fluids of life through its wounds. The dying Jesus himself is enough to shatter any order we might try to force on death.

And if we remind ourselves that, for Christians, the dying man is the Son of God, who will be our judge, and who calls us to follow him to that cross and to die that death, he shatters any and all of our attempts at order with absolute authority, beyond all argument and objection. The image of that cross was traced on my forehead before I was a month old. That we're not all overwhelmed by this image of human pain is probably just one more instance, evident enough in our numbness to the world's daily misery, but here the crowning instance, of our power to blind ourselves.

There are some parts of the Christian family that orbit more about the victorious Christ or that scrub the crosses clean of the foul human mess. In the church I attend now, the crosses are only shapes. (Our processional cross has an extremely stylized and *fully robed* human figure on it.) You would have to be told what happened on them and what they were for. The same would be true of all the Lutheran churches I served as a pastor. We worshipped facing the image of a cross, not the image of a crucifixion.

The experience of my Roman Catholic childhood was far different: the thorns, the nails, and the spear, the scourging and the blood, were not just spoken of and sung about but shown and seen. The Stations of the Cross, the devotional service with a set of fourteen meditations and prayers on Jesus's way to death, from his condemnation to the tomb, was a highlight of Lent. I remember how endless they seemed to me on hot Friday nights in spring, following the priest around the packed church from station to station. But the images of the Stations were always up, year round, for private use of the rite. In the free-for-all services of my youth, before Vatican II worked to regain the communal nature of the Mass, it was rare to attend a Mass, especially on weekdays, without seeing one or more people making their own cycle of the Stations while the priest mumbled at the altar.

But there was one rite in my church that I've personally never seen elsewhere and that, for years, I assumed was a local tradition cherished and transplanted by the Poles from the Old Country. But it flourished widely in Medieval Europe, and it's not really that uncommon. It's called the Veneration of the Cross. It was done on Good Friday afternoon and it brought the crucified Lord even closer to us. Like many large Roman Catholic churches, there were centers for private devotion all over the nave and, on the back wall, there was what I at least remember as a life-sized, excruciatingly detailed image of the crucified Jesus, fastened to a cross that was certainly scaled down, since the wood barely stretched beyond his limbs. On Good Friday, this crucifix was taken to the front and set lying across the steps of the altar, with a priest kneeling on each side, armed with a napkin. Then the congregation would come up the central aisle, which, as I've noted, was quite long. We didn't so much process as just moved raggedly forward together. People would be mumbling prayers, you could see lots of rosaries swinging from clasped hands. At a designated point, you went on your knees and moved forward that way. The truly pious ones would take the entire aisle on their knees. When you got to the nearly naked body of Jesus, you leaned forward and kissed it. You put your mouth on the image of flesh about to rot. Then you rose and left as the priest wiped away the touch of your lips with his napkin.

The physical aspect of this ceremony has remained so intensely vivid to me that I have no memory of any prayers or hymns associated with it at all. I only remember the long, shuffling movement up the aisle, the hardness of the floor on my knees, the rustle of clothing and quiet voices.

I see this now as one extreme way, but a way closely bound to the rest of the life of faith, that the reality of death entered me, in some way beneath what I could think or feel at the time. And yet I do remember feeling challenged to kiss, not just the body, but the wounds themselves and not being able to make myself do it.

III

There was another way death was in my life, a way that was as shallow and ignorant as I was. It came to me on television and in the movies.

This was the bloodless death of melodrama, where bullets seem to have as little force as slaps, where they don't shatter faces or tear bodies apart or cause gaping wounds hemorrhaging blood, where a mortal shot is like the turning off of a switch, leaving the human machine time to stagger a bit or speak a word of farewell, the bloodless death the film directors of my adult life devoted much effort to make as bloody as possible.

This was in the early fifties and I suppose I was among the first generation of all-day television watchers. At the time, much of the programming available to me was made up of Hollywood movies from the thirties and forties: I watched gangsters, cops, private detectives, soldiers, sailors, pilots, cowboys, gunfighters, and the U.S. Cavalry lead dangerous and thrilling lives of aspiration, adventure, comradeship, and, sometimes, sacrifice, always noble and never regretted.

The deaths in these movies were the deaths of stories and they hid a deeper and more insidious bloodless lie. Death was part of an exciting life, part of dangerous occupations, part of any dangerous circumstance that might come upon you; as part of that life, it came with a meaning, it came ordered and defined by moral values. Innocent people died because evil people wanted what they had; guilty people died because good people punished them; good people died to sacrifice themselves for others. These things can be painful, even horrible, but they're not senseless. Death comes with a meaning and purpose. These, too, the storytellers of my time have worked to make more complex, more confused and confusing, less aglow with sense, meaning, purpose.

But, at the time, though I probably saw several deaths depicted every day, I saw nothing of the disorders of life, neither the riot and chaos of the mangled body nor the twisting, the corruption, or the sheer wounding of the spirit brought by violent death. I had no idea of the horror of a life ending senselessly.

Oddly enough, I had a special interest in war movies, driven by my father's service in World War II, but I had in him as well a witness to the realities of death, a witness outwardly whole but, I only realized much later, marked and disturbed in spirit by what he'd lived through. I saw him as glamorous through the movies rather than seeing the movies as hollow and unreal through him. I only began to see him clearly later, when I saw him through the furious and explicit stories of the Vietnam War, stories with no respect for polite illusions.

IV

But it was by my father that I first learned how death could jolt people out of their normal lives; it was in him that I first saw how death could scatter and blur someone into an unrecognizable shape.

Part of what I now think the war did to my father was to root him more deeply and desperately to the life he had, or dreamed he had, before it. Much to my mother's fury, and to my increasing bewilderment, all his siblings owned their own homes while we lived in cramped rooms above his parents. It was an old house, not really designed for two separate families, and all our comings and goings were through the living space and under the relentless observation of my grandparents. I grew up with the sense of inhabiting the corners of someone else's life.

My grandfather spoke English with an accent so thick it was incomprehensible to me. He smoked a pipe, and his pipe rack of dark wood now holds my pencils and scribbled notes. In my memory, he is always wearing a three-piece suit and always seems to be standing up and looking down on me. I remember being almost terrified of approaching him for anything; certainly I would never do it without being commanded to. It wasn't fear so much as a sense that he was too far above me to be bothered by me: like our senior pastor, or the pope. As a child, I assumed all others, even my father, would see my grandfather the same way: distant, at a height above us, unknowable, uncomfortable to be near.

One evening I was playing in the little hallway at the top of the steps that led to our rooms. I must have been fairly young, since I could barely see over the sill of the window that overlooked the backyard. The weather must have been nice, since my grandparents were sitting out in the yard, a reason for me to stay inside. My father was looking out the window. He was either playing with me or talking with me, because I remember the sense of the two of us being involved in something together when, all at once, he spun off into a different world. He cried out, it was as though I no longer existed, and he was running frantically down the stairs. He was blind to me, he was moving faster and more recklessly than I had ever seen him move, he was out of my sight, and I didn't know what had happened or what to do. I have a memory of straining to see what was happening and seeing my grandfather falling over, but he must have fallen already before I was able to do that. I later learned he had something called a stroke. Oddly, I have no memory of my father appearing below me or reaching him, no memory either of my mother or anyone else being around. The pictures in my memory end with me alone, at the top of the stairs.

It was as though my father had leaped out of my world into his father's world, leaving me behind. He had become someone else, someone new to me, with a life bound to his own father that I had never imagined. It was the haste that shocked me; I have a blurry image of him passing before me, wearing a white t-shirt; it was like just being missed in the street by a car or a bicycle that you didn't see coming, something as unaware of you as you were of it.

I recall almost nothing else from that time. It was the first death of someone close to me, but I don't recall how long my grandfather lingered, if I was taken to see him in the hospital, how he got there, if I was at the wake, or the funeral, or the funeral lunch, or how my grandmother acted as she lost him.

I might have been excluded from what was going on, the way children commonly were then. (I remember hearing—or overhearing, in whispers—of one aunt who died of cancer. In fact, I remember the word itself always being whispered or silently mouthed, as though the absent one who had it was already entombed, or as though fatal illness was something you could catch through language.) Even when I was serving as a pastor, there were some families who worked to shield their children from death. I would often hear: "They don't understand." Unlike, I would think, the rest of us.

But I wonder now if the reason I have no awareness of anything else is that I was so overwhelmed by the change in my father: the way he was swept away that first moment, and then, in the wake of the death, how silent he became, how withdrawn, how he had no time or attention for anything else, for me.

He had always told me bedtime stories, usually of his time in the war, and these are the first days I recall of him not coming to my bed before I slept. I can see myself going to my mother and wanting her to explain why he wouldn't come tell me a story.

She did give me the explanation that explains everything and nothing: "His daddy just died so he wants to be alone."

Vaguely aware I was being a pest, vaguely aware of how pointless my question was, I asked, "But why?" She told me to go to bed.

I think no matter how many hands we hold, how many eyes we look into, how many arms embrace us in sympathy, death will always have the power to isolate us, to leave us lonely, inside our own wandering thoughts, inside our own storming or drifting feelings, inside ourselves.

V

I would come to think of what my father presented me with as a common, natural response to death's coming, from the first shocked panic to the later, lonely silence. There's a kind of purity or simplicity to it: we note a loss, we see a person feeling and absorbing that loss. There's an uncomplicated clarity to the values expressed. But there are harsher, wilder, stranger responses provoked by death.

I was older when my mother's mother died. My mother was, in the best of times, far from the stoicism of my father. I often thought of her as living in her own silent opera, breaking into emotional arias of sorrow, fury, or delight at the slightest nudge of circumstance. So I was prepared for a louder and more dramatic brooding, more tears, more memories recounted in laughter and pain, more exclamations of what could no longer be. And so it happened.

But there was one moment I wasn't prepared for. We were gathered at the funeral home on the morning of the funeral, ready to be driven together to the church where the priest would meet us at the door for the entrance rite. There was the last viewing, some prayers, then the coffin was closed, and we all proceeded outside.

We had gathered in a rough circle around the coffin as the funeral director was maneuvering it to the hearse, when my mother broke from the circle, threw herself on top of the coffin, and beat on it with her fists, wailing, "Don't go! Ma! Don't go! Don't leave me!"

I can't remember responding in any way but stunned contemplation. It was an eruption of wounded and outraged life, a scream of protest against nature itself, and it froze us all into uncomprehending witnesses. No one moved, no one spoke, we only watched. Even the funeral director stood still, at a loss for some way to proceed. I'm not sure how long she lay weeping and pounding on the coffin: it's one of those moments that exist in their own swollen time. Finally, my father walked slowly to her, took her arm gently, patted her back, and quietly said, "C'mon. Let's go." And she slipped off the coffin and went with him.

I've never been able to decide what was driving her that morning, why, instead of sobbing in my father's arms, or her older sister's arms, or clutching my sister to her, she hurled herself so far out of the normal customs of grief. I can't believe she actually thought she could call her mother back to life, but I've wondered if the thought of her mother's death was so unacceptable to her, so raw a threat of abandonment, so deep a violation of life and of goodness, that she just burst past all sense to scream for what she wanted most. I've wondered, too, if she were revealing how alone she felt with only the rest of us. I've sometimes thought, more harshly, or impatiently, I guess, that she was partly acting the role of wild grief, that she needed to be seen going beyond what everyone else was doing. Still, I suppose I'm thinking of a need that was beyond reason, desperate, uncontrollable.

I could say that what she did had the same clarity of value that my father's actions had: we note a loss, we see a person feeling and, here, refusing to accept that loss. It would be an extreme example of grief, but an example different in degree, not in kind.

And yet it revealed to me a well of mystery within us, a raging of the spirit's desires, refusals, hurts and terrors, something not pure or simple or uncomplicated, but something as mixed, shaded, and mysterious as anything else we do.

VI

I went to high school as a boarding student in a Benedictine monastery. In the four years I was there, the entire community would usually attend the funerals of the monks who died, among whom were a couple of our teachers. The monastery had a substantial amount of land on the Illinois River, and we would process after the funeral, with six hooded monks bearing the coffin, through the woods surrounding the main building to a little cemetery on a small rise. I recall playing the trombone in a brass choir that accompanied one of these processions. I sometimes say I went to high school in the thirteenth century and this is one of the memories that move me to say that.

The monks tended mostly to be silent and distant. If there was great grief or any emotional display, it wasn't shown to us. The very strong sense was that those who died had simply reached the land they had spent their lives journeying to, that the final vows they took in their youth had begun their dying. In many ways, these deaths reminded me of the deaths I attended as an acolyte. There was the same thrill of liberation from the drudgery of classes, and, in themselves, they were simply the deaths of the old. Even the teacher we knew the best seemed old, or at least mortally tired, to us: a capable, competent man, he acquired more jobs in the community each year. I remember another student saying the monastery had worked him to death.

But then, when I was a senior, our prefect died, and this was something different. Each boarding class, each year, was overseen by two prefects, usually younger monks, and usually strict, some, I thought, to the point of sadism. One of them was always with us outside of classes, and they took turns sleeping in a little curtained-off nook in our dormitories. At 6:30 a.m., they woke us with a large handbell as they walked down the aisles between our beds. If you were slow to stir, you might get hit with the bell. After lights-out, they would, from time to time, silently drift down the aisles in the dark, like ghosts in black robes. Being with them from sunrise to sunset, like them or not, we became closer to them than to the other monks.

Senior year, however, was a year of privilege. Instead of a dormitory on the third floor and a study hall on another, with our clothing lockers in the basement, we lived in our own wing just off the main floor, four of us to a room. We had our own balcony with our own entrance. And we had only one prefect who left us pretty much to ourselves and had little interest in organizing games to keep us occupied. He probably couldn't have stood the boredom.

Father Ralph was one of those teachers and leaders students are dazzled by: loud, irreverent, funny, flamboyant, he dominated any group he joined. He could crack the whip as well as any other prefect, but seldom had to. We liked him too much and didn't want to disappoint him. We adored him.

Instead of a handbell to wake us, he would wheel his record player into the hallway, turn up the volume, and, at 6:30 sharp, he would blast out something rousing, like "The Stars and Stripes Forever" or, one of his favorites, "The Night They Invented Champagne" from *Gigi*. (Whenever I hear it, I still see his record player blaring just outside his door.)

I had a friend who was a natural early riser and was usually the first person to the washroom, usually beating the bell. For whatever reason, either because he was having trouble sleeping or because he simply wanted a backup, Father Ralph delegated Fred to enter his room and make sure he was moving.

One morning I woke to silence. I remember coming slowly out of my room into the hallway. It's a very dream-like memory: I seem to be gliding; no one else is around but other students must have been up and moving. I was standing outside Father Ralph's door, staring at it. It opened, Fred stepped out, and quickly closed the door behind him. I think I asked him what was going on. He stared at me silently, then hurried out of our wing without a word. My memory, once again, leaves me standing there.

Father Ralph had died in his sleep. It was like losing a parent. None of us had seen much of our parents for three years or so; some of my classmates had been in boarding schools for ten years. To live under some pretty harsh, authoritarian figures for those years, to finally be given a leader who brings you joy, then to lose him suddenly is quite a blow. I've sometimes looked back and thought we got little help dealing with the loss, but I'm not sure, even now, what help would be.

I have no memory of when or how we were told of his death. Apart from one blurry image of filing past his coffin at the wake, I remember very little of anything else that had to do with losing him. But there are two things that remain strongly with me from later that same morning.

The first memory is also dream-like, almost trance-like. There were about thirty of us senior boarders and I see us all in the dark hallway moving slowly, almost floating, in silence, round and round for hours. We drift out to the porch, which also seems unnaturally dark, then drift back in. No one seems to be speaking. I know all the boys floating around me but they appear to me as strangers. I don't look into any faces I can recognize. We're all moving, constantly, but time isn't moving. We're like children under a spell. I suppose we really were: the spell of death.

I have a strong sense of having no idea what to do, what to say, where to go, whom to seek out: life just seems to have stopped. I've seen people get frantic in the wake of death, inventing pointless tasks for themselves if they couldn't find something that needed doing. Looking back, I've thought that someone should have forced us to do something instead of leaving us to ourselves, but, for all I know, someone might have tried. They might have even succeeded in getting us to do something I can't remember. My trance-like image of darkness, helplessness, and loneliness needs no source beyond a wounded spirit.

But we must have been alone and drifting by ourselves at some time that morning because my second strong memory could only have happened without the presence of some adult authority figure. (In fairness, I imagine the other monks might have been as stunned as we were.)

In this memory, I'm now in a group that's brooding on our porch. I can sense something already familiar to me: the edginess and volatile anger of aimless young men who feel hurt or cheated or under attack. I recognize the boys shifting and pacing around me but, strangely, they were the ones I knew least in my class, the ones I was most distant from. Some of them I actively avoided because of their belligerence. I can't believe none of my friends were anywhere near, so this too must be an image shaped emotionally by an isolating wound.

Then a car came down the drive and parked by the porch. Two or three students got out of the car and came running up the stone steps. They too were senior boarders who, for some reason now lost to me, had been on some sort of trip that morning; I can't remember if they had left early and not been told of the death or if they had been gone overnight. As they ran up to us, the first student, Charlie, jarred us all by his obvious excitement and delight. It was that horrible moment when someone bubbling with innocent joy blunders unknowingly into an arena of tragedy. Worse, this boy was, though not the least popular, somewhat outside the dominant groups of the class, one of the easier targets for bullying and ridicule, someone unlikely to be granted grace for a mistake. He shouted, laughing, "Where's Father Ralph? He's just got to hear this! Where is he? Where's Father Ralph?"

The boy standing next to me, one I admired for his athletic looks and smooth style, but someone I was wary of because of his quick temper, exploded. Next to him, I thought I could feel him rising into the air, glowing with heat, swelling with fury. In an instant, he was at the top of the steps, screaming down at the happy boy. "He's dead! He's dead! You can't tell him anything! He's dead!"

Poor Charlie's face twisted into stunned misery. He looked around at the rest of us, looking for understanding. Maybe he was looking for help. I think everybody was frozen by the outburst. Finally, someone more self-possessed than I was said quietly, "He died this morning. Um—in his sleep. We don't—that's all we know." Then the rage settled a bit and people started talking to each other.

I thought it was one of the most unjust and cruel attacks I had ever seen. In boarding school, you tend always to be on the alert for attacks from any quarter, so I could easily imagine myself stepping into the same horrible encounter. The angry boy had simply assumed a moral high ground from nothing more than his own bitter knowledge. He assumed the right to punish anyone in sight, for mere ignorance, for merely being there, for giving him something to rage at.

Looking back, from a half-century on, I hear those same words from that same boy as a cry of absolute misery that finally found a way to leap out of him: "He's dead. He's lost to us. None of us can see him, touch him, tell or be told anything again. He's dead." Understanding it doesn't make it easier to take.

I've come to see this, too, as a common, natural response to death: misery that can't emerge unless it turns itself into some kind of rage: senseless outbursts, angry demands, crazy ultimatums, even physical assaults, all the worse because the rage will never give us what we lost. The loss allows us to claim authority and freedom to act. We're fleeing the helplessness of incurable suffering.

I've been tempted to call this a common male response to loss but I've seen women react this way as well. I think I've seen it most in capable people who are used to taking charge, the actors and the helpers, the fixers and the deciders. It unnerves me most in men because I'm so used to male emotion threatening violence. Men seem less able than women to sit with the dying and accept their helplessness, unable even to remain in the same room. I recall some of the men I've sat with in hospitals rising quickly and rushing out. I've heard them invent every pretext to be elsewhere. Seeing their physical agitation in my memory, I can easily imagine them smashing chairs against the wall. I've wanted to smash a few myself.

When I was on internship, first visiting homes and hospitals, my supervisor tried to make sure I experienced most of the ordinary sides of parish ministry. Though he presided at all the funerals while I assisted, he made sure I shared in the regular visits to the seriously ill and the dying.

One of them, Ellen, was a very active member of our congregation, well beloved, a leader of the women's group, who was dying of an inoperable brain tumor. Through the year, I dropped in on a journey I would accompany, with one person or another, for the rest of my active life: the journey from the early days of care, when the stricken ones are still cheerful, lively, a little bemused, hopeful, to the last days of waiting without hope, when they are almost unrecognizable, twisted, shrunken, beyond action and thought.

Though Ellen was an active member, her husband, not unusually, hardly ever appeared at the church. So, when I walked into the hospital, not only did I look young and, no doubt, unqualified, I was pretty much a stranger to him. While his spouse, in the early days, greeted me happily, he had to put up with someone he scarcely knew on some of the worst days of his life. This probably didn't help the dynamics in the room.

As things got worse and Ellen was less able to communicate, the silence in the room, always uncomfortable, then painful as it filled with the approach of death, would sometimes become unbearable. Pointless and trivial conversation, then, would appear like a rescue ship to castaways. But the words seemed to dissolve in the air.

One day, near the end, I sighed and turned to my brooding companion and said, "So how about you? How are you doing?"

It looked like fire was coming out of his eyes. "Me? Me? How am *I* doing?" he shouted. "There's nothing wrong with me!" He stabbed his finger at the bed. "There! Right there! There's the problem! See it? There's the problem!"

His violence was shouting something else, but he couldn't bear to admit, at least to the young stranger I was, how much of himself was dying too. It was one of the times that made me wonder if I really wanted to accept this as my vocation.

I remember another man who insisted, quietly this time, that he had no problem accepting his mother's death: she had a long life and died peacefully. He had several brothers and he was the one who made all the funeral planning easy. Then, the night of the wake, he never showed up. He wasn't at the church for the last viewing before the funeral director closed the coffin. He arrived just in time for the service and sat with his brothers in the pew, but he looked at and talked to no one, never joined in the prayers, never even glanced toward the altar. He gazed intently, through the entire service, at the closed coffin, as though his mother had hypnotized him before she died and was never going to let him wake up.

PART TWO

Bodies and Rites: Serving

I

I have been speaking of the different ways I learned about death and what it can bring upon us. The scenes and images that have risen from my memory are random and unrelated but they reflect the essential disorder of death, its intrusion into our time and across our paths. My memories of the deaths I attended as a pastor have the same quality: sometimes I recall a hospital visit, sometimes a moment in the funeral itself, or something a sister said, or the surprising laugh of a spouse at an old story. One great difference, however, is that, during my service as a pastor, death became a defining part of my life: as a regular and expected intrusion, as a task and a call to attend, as something that needed me to enter its arena and speak the words of human sympathy and, beyond them, the words of faith. I had no idea, when I first thought of entering the seminary, how great a part of my life this would be.

The parishes Mary Carol and I served were old parishes in stable communities. Serving them, you could see and feel the shape of life over time, its growth and decay, all the threads that wind through generations, the gifts and the sins of the elders working in the young, in a way larger or more transient places don't allow. Cemeteries, marking out the visible horizon of life, were as much or more a part of them as any other ordered human space: neither of the towns we lived in had hospitals and one no longer had a school. But they both had cemeteries and one of them had two. The first thing I saw when I looked out the front window on the first morning in our first parish was the cemetery across the street from the parsonage. At our second parish, there was a cemetery on each side of the town: you could go from one to the other in an easy morning's walk.

The community could watch itself moving toward death. You could see all the well-known and active leaders aging and being replaced. You could see the young growing, being wounded, aging themselves. You could watch people's steps slowing in the street, then see them appear with canes or walkers, then see them no more. In church, the faces in the pews grew wrinkled, hair turned gray, bodies bent and stiffened.

All this kept death close. The presence of the aging and the dying brought that horizon closer to everyone, for good or ill. It somehow clarified life or completed its frame.

(The first church I was active in as an adult was near Purdue University and the congregation, except for a few older professors, was mostly made up of students and younger professors on their way elsewhere. There was a lot of turnover: students graduated, professors sought and found new positions, military families moved in and out in a year or two. But these were active lives moving on; all the extended families, parents and siblings, were elsewhere; we were all young and healthy and independent. I was going to say no one was dying but the real difference was: nobody had to notice we were all dying and would all be dead some day. A serious illness got everyone's attention. One of the professors, neither very young nor very old, did sicken and die in my time there, and it stunned all of us. It was as though some horrible curse had singled him out. I remember how hard it was to accept that death was really going to come to him, that he would really never leave the hospital. He seemed, in his sickness, to have entered some other life, unwanted, weaker, uglier, rather than revealing the nature of the life we all shared.)

As a pastor, serving parishes like those we served, you're privileged to be invited into all the ways death can come, from the sudden, shocking deaths of the young to the long, agonizing dying of the old. But you enter them with a split consciousness: you see and feel the grief and the loss; but you're always aware of the choices that have to be made, the things that have to be done. Something in me was always noting moments or events I might touch on in my sermon, biblical passages that might bring a light to this death, hymns that might lift these mourners to peace. If I were lucky, some would come to me. (In the same way, when I attended the funeral, in another church, of someone I'd known, I would helplessly be thinking, moment after moment, of how I would have done it differently.) Even when someone you've known well dies, however much you feel the impact, you never forget you have a task to attend to.

Yet the balance of this split consciousness does shift over time when you're serving the same parish. You never can feel what the closest mourners feel, but you feel more as the years make the place and the people more your own. The professional distance fades as the personal flows into it. Also, as each gathering of mourners begins to move toward healing, you move into the next death and the next and the next. This can be quite a weight when the funerals come clustered together, as they sometimes do.

Mortal illness and death always bring isolation, a shrinking of life to just a few people, one or two rooms. You feel like you're living under a dome that's getting smaller and smaller. At times, I started to feel like I was burying my parents and my grandparents over and over again. I would look at people and wonder when they would die. I was helplessly writing a funeral sermon in my head for everyone I knew. If I looked at photographs, even of new babies or of kids at a recent party, I'd see them as dead people.

I realized once that I was half-consciously thinking of myself as ten or so years older than I really was. At the worst of these times, anything I thought of planning seemed futile to me: I was sure I'd die before I could finish it.

Usually, the funerals clear out, some other things or other people call to you, you return to living, but the weight of grief remains a burden, even a hazard, until you leave for some new place or find something else to do with your life.

II

The deaths that gave me the most anxiety were those I had to approach with even more ignorance than usual: the families who regarded themselves as members but most of whom I'd never met; those with no church connections anywhere who still felt the need for a church funeral; elderly members who'd been gone for years but needed to be buried near their grandparents. Once we got a phone message—before the days of cell phones—telling us a body was on the way from Ohio by train and we should be ready to do the funeral in two days. Not even our most elderly members remembered the deceased or his family. (At least, in that case, the surviving family left all the details to us. It's harder to deal with utter strangers who radiate their distrust of you and who are often outraged when they can't dictate what will and what will not be in the service.)

I can still clearly see, in my memory, a door I was approaching one Sunday morning, and it might as well have been an impenetrable wall, for all I could imagine of what was behind it: a home I'd never been to where a man I'd never met had died suddenly during the night, and I'd been asked to go out to the family, whom I'd never met either, gathered there in shock. I had been preaching that morning at a church where we were filling in while they called a new pastor. The family had called the church just before the service, asking if someone could come out. They were well known to the congregation, well thought of and well liked, but I hadn't met them yet in the short time that I'd been there. The only thing I remember from my painful presence in that stunned living room was the wife marveling how warm the bed still was when she woke to find her husband not breathing. But when I walked to that door I could have been walking off the end of the earth, or stepping out of life itself.

Some of us at seminary were once discussing the challenges of funerals with one of the pastoral counseling professors; he allowed that meeting with strangers to plan funerals was tough, but he pointed out meeting with parishioners who dislike you intensely (and may have been avoiding church until a death forced their return) could be much worse. Having done both, I think I'd still rather deal with people I knew, however hostile. I'd like to say that sometimes a funeral would offer a way toward reconciliation, but, just as often, it could be the last completed task that allowed a final break. Those were far from the easiest moments of my life. But at least I knew what I was facing and, really, so did the family. I knew, at least, that they accepted the church's funeral traditions, or they would have gone elsewhere.

But I think what gives peculiar weight to these encounters, what heightens our discomfort with one another, our strangeness to each other, is the unwanted, uncomfortable strangeness of death itself. There's a darkness that closes around everything before us: we're jolted from the blind trust that tomorrow will be like today; we see it won't, so we see nothing. Death becomes a black sun, revealing our own ignorance and the horrifying uncertainty of all things.

III

As I went from hospital room to hospital room, from death to death, something I'd always carry with me and the first thing I'd grab when I got an emergency call was my thin, green leather *Occasional Services* book, one of the most useful volumes my church body ever produced and one worth knowing well. It contained a surprisingly broad variety of possible services, from the blessing of a civil marriage to thanksgiving at the retirement of a debt, from the setting apart of a deaconess to guidelines for ringing church bells. All these came with appropriate prayers and lists of suggested biblical passages and hymns, all handily indexed by topic at the back. But what I treasured it for were the services surrounding illness and death, the selected passages of promise and comfort, and the thoughtfully composed prayers for moments of pain, turmoil, loss. This book was my proof of identification, not telling others who I was but reminding me who I was. It was my staff and shield (or my security blanket), my torch in the night, my sword in the battle.

I know pastors who scorn formal prayers and insist on praying freely out of whatever the moment presents. Well, I've done that, too, but I grew up in and served in highly formal and liturgical traditions. I find strength in sharing prayers that have been spoken by Christians before me, through ages of faith. Also, I've been there when some of those freely praying pastors have prayed and they tended, not always, but often enough, to "just ask, Lord," for the same thing in the same way I heard them the last time. And formal prayer can bring a breadth of concern we might not reach on our own. The Lord's Prayer, for example, sets us to ask for God's will to be done and our sins to be forgiven, reminding us as well to forgive those who sin against us. You might think, when death is coming, that it's not God's will but our own that we want done and that our sins are the last thing we care to think about. But to pray "Thy will be done" brings a summons to rise up and stand fast, accepting what must come. And one of death's dark powers is setting our sins to rage and gnaw away within us.

I sometimes carried a pocket Bible, too, but I usually brought it only when I had a chance to mark the passages I would use beforehand—in other words, when I was visiting the known, not the unknown. For one thing, the nimbleness of my fingers was no match for its thin pages, especially when searching for passages under stress. Also, using more than one passage required another clumsy search. My *Occasional Services* book not only had thicker pages (and three thick ribbon markers) but it had pointed groupings of treasured passages, surrounded as well with short prayers that could stir up and support my tired or troubled mind. One of the most worn sections in my book holds, in three consecutive pages, Psalm 121, Romans 8, and John 14. My favorite page, perhaps the one I used the most, had the five short passages of reassurance and peace used in our worship book's Compline service, passages I read to myself almost every night.

But there were as well passages I wouldn't use, that I could not imagine using: the healing of Simon's mother; the summary statements of Jesus or the twelve laying on hands, anointing, and healing "many," or even "each one" who was brought; the admonition from James to gather the elders of the church around anyone sick for prayer and anointing, with the promise that "the prayer offered in faith will make the sick one well." Those pages in my book are not very well worn. I couldn't make that promise. I know this sounds ludicrously fastidious, but I was sometimes even hesitant to use John 11, "I am the Resurrection and the Life," because it reminds everyone of the raising of Lazarus, the gift that so many desperate mourners want and that none are going to get.

Of course, I prayed for health and healing, but I wasn't primarily there to bring or to call down a cure, and I feared suggesting that I might be. I was there to bring the life of the gospel, to be, together with those there, the body of Christ in that place, to summon them, even in the bed of sickness, even in the house of death, to be Christian witnesses. I didn't come to finally do what medical skill had failed to do. But not all pastors saw things that way.

I was visiting the local hospital one day, on my way out, when I saw an older man I knew sitting silently, head down, next to the bed of his son. His son, lying still, was close to my age. I knocked softly and asked if I could stop a moment.

He was from a large family I knew very well. Two of his brothers, with *their* large families, were regular members of our church, and I had met most of the others over the years at all the rites of passage: baptisms, marriages, anniversaries, funerals. Some pastors in our small town made a point of dropping in on everyone in the hospital. (In the early days of my service, unimaginable now, there was an open book on the counter of the information desk. You'd see pastors standing there copying down every name and room number.) I tried to avoid this, as a matter of professional ethics. But it was hard to walk past people you knew well, so I always tried to be clear I was stopping as a friend, not as a pastor. That wasn't always so easy either. But this man I did know very well, and liked, so I stepped in when he smiled and nodded, and I quietly pulled a chair next to him.

His son was going to die. He lay there, barely breathing, shrunken and ravaged by cancer. His body was curled into itself, collapsing into itself. He had been dying in that room for a while. In those days, before hospice care, hospitals were kept full and vigils like this were common. The young man had gone from an active life to his death bed before many people were aware how ill he was, or how swiftly cancer could destroy a life. So, if he was yours, you sat there and sat there and watched the suffering and hoped the pain could be eased. It's a miserable vigil for anybody, but for a parent watching a grown child, so recently vibrant with achievement and possibility, it's slow torture that won't even end for you with the child's death.

I could never, in that small town, not be a pastor, so, instead of talking like ordinary men, probably avoiding, like men, anything very serious, the father began to speak to me about his strong faith and how much he leaned on it. He told me how much he appreciated the frequent visits of his own pastor, someone I had a few reservations about, but I was glad to hear it. I like to see people come through when they have to, and shared moments of pain can form strong bonds.

Then the father started talking about miracles. I stayed silent but, once he got going, I may as well not have been there. He was staring into a future he hoped he could create, reciting a litany of unearthly, groundless hope. He seemed to know a lot about miracles.

It slowly came to me that this was what, just then, he was leaning on his faith for: the miracle that would make his son rise up and walk back to his life. It came to me that this was why he appreciated his pastor's visits so much: he was the one person that would speak to him explicitly, authoritatively, and at great length, of the only thing he wanted: a miracle of healing. Maybe his pastor even believed he could provide one somehow. But it's my belief that faith needs to have something else to say at a time like that.

I can still see that suffering man, leaning forward on his chair, saying, "We know there are different kinds of miracles . . . ," telling them off on his fingers as he looked at the floor, as though reciting by rote a lesson he couldn't quite grasp the sense of.

I sat there silently, wanting to scream, wanting to strangle that pastor. I reflected that religion has always been able to find ways to make earthly torture worse.

I did pray with him when I left. I like to think I prayed for love shared, for light in the dark, for courage and strength, for union with the crucified one who wondered why God had forsaken him. It would have been a typical prayer for me at a time like that.

I didn't pray for a miracle. None came, and the young man died.

IV

The most wrenching and the most frightening hospital moments were, of course, the emergencies, the accidents. Those frantic trips, driven by fear driven by love, strip us down to what we treasure in the rush for help. I stepped into an emergency room one Saturday in my yard clothes, looking, I imagine now, like a shiftless derelict, to meet one of the most elegant women I knew, running toward me, weeping and disheveled, hair streaming wildly, covered with blood. Before the reality of why we were there, appearances were meaningless.

And yet, the emergencies brought within them a strange flicker of hope. The rush for help is also driven by the blind faith that help will do some good, that it will bring healing. Especially with the accidents of the young, we're looking for the restoration of life, and there's an edginess, even an eagerness, to our waiting. It's not like the waiting around the beds where hope slowly dies and people start praying for the end.

In the first year my wife and I attended seminary, our small son was hit by a car just outside our house, knocked right out of one of his shoes and thrown sixty-nine feet down the street. I remember both the desperation and the hope, probably itself based on nothing but desperate wanting, when the ambulance finally arrived, then took off for the hospital. We finally got, later that day, a firm enough assurance of his recovery to settle our worst fears. Then we entered our own existential introduction to things we would be watching people go through for all the years of our service: being confused and shut out, feeling helpless, powerless, needing to wait and wait and wait to see your loved one, sometimes only for a few minutes before you're physically locked out of the intensive care unit again.

The hospital in Minneapolis had its own, unique confusions: many levels, many corridors, many streets outside. I remember coming out of a strange entrance late one night and having no idea where I was or how to find my car. One of the most useful things the hospital chaplains did for me some days was give me directions, even walking me out; this was one of the unplanned lessons in being a pastor I was thankful for.

But all hospitals, even the smallest, are bewildering, especially to worried and frightened people. Look down any corridor, lined with closed doors on each side. It's clear to the nurses, it's clear to the technicians and the janitors, what each room holds. But every corridor and every door looks alike to you. It's like being in one of the horror movies where you never see the monster: your imagination runs wild.

Even when you can see something or can watch a procedure, you don't know what you're looking at or how to take it. The first time I visited someone in a ward for neck and spinal injuries, I thought the people I could glimpse as I walked past their rooms would never return to anything like a normal life. Yet I met one of them on the street several weeks later, cheerful and pretty thoroughly recovered. On the other hand, I once visited a lively young woman who sat cross-legged on her bed and chattered happily about everything under the sun. You might have wondered why she was in a hospital room at all, but she was beyond hope and we soon did her funeral.

In the last years of my service, a couple of the hospitals I visited regularly began using senior volunteers as guides. They'd join you at the information desk (or even help you find the information desk), then walk you far enough to make sure you wouldn't get lost. Along the way, they were blessedly eager to display their knowledge of hospital ways, how things were done and what might be on offer for your comfort. More importantly, they brought a welcome human presence, the companion and guide every anxious pilgrim hopes to meet.

I think it's true as well that, towards the end of my service, doctors in general became more communicative, but this may be something that varies greatly with each person's experience, and I've met at least one young couple who told me I was wrong. To return to our son's hospital stay, we were gathered the afternoon of the accident around his bed with a neurologist and one of the nurses. Our son had taken a serious blow to the head, and the doctor was doing tests. At one point, he got my attention when he ran his thumbnail up the bottom of Jon's foot. I remembered just reading about this test in a biography of Steven Biko, the South African activist beaten to death by the police, and I was sick with apprehension because I couldn't remember what was a good and what was a bad reaction. I watched the doctor's face but it was a mask. Then he nodded once, turned without speaking, and walked to the end of the room. In my memory, that room seems as long as a football field. He stopped when he reached the door and silently beckoned the nurse to him. She hurried to his side, he whispered to her briefly, then left. She hurried back to us, looking down. I was choking with dread. She leaned across the bed, and she whispered, "The doctor says he'll be just fine."

This being my measure of medical communication, I suppose when I sat with families who were being given any information at all, as well as being allowed to ask questions, that I probably would see that as a vast improvement.

Still, in these awful moments, there is no avoiding helplessness, fear, blindness. Our desperation to be told anything is heightened because we can do nothing. I've come to see our ignorant waiting in the wake of serious injury, in the face of death or crippling loss, as an essentially revealing moment, a time when we're made to suffer through, without protective illusions, the truth of our place within the shape and the forces of creation.

But you learn how important it is to be physically near one another, to be able to see and to touch each other. Visiting one young man whose immune system was devastated, we had to wear surgical gowns, gloves, and masks. I had never felt so inexpressive or so diminished. Encased in that costume, I felt as though I'd forgotten how to speak.

It's the denial of presence, the necessary prohibition of physical nearness, that gives a special anxiety to the intensive care waiting rooms. It's not hard to accept the reality, the need for the healers to keep the patient relatively isolated while they watched and worked; you just can't forget it's not the reality you want. The minutes when you're allowed, in extremely limited numbers, to visit, or just to see, your loved one are as nothing compared to the hours upon hours you spend in the waiting room. You spend the hours because you want to be there, as close as you can be; but all the time makes you feel painfully how much more you want. It's like knowing someone's suffering just out of your reach and not being able to do anything about it. And, of course, that's exactly what it is, and you can't.

I brought my own difficulties to this anguished arena, inseparable from my calling. As a pastor, I was automatically granted the great privilege of being there at all. Even the strictest nurses would grant me passage. One Sunday afternoon, exhausted and stressed, called to the hospital for an emergency, wondering how bad it was, I was hurrying down the hall when a nurse, who was no doubt also having a bad day, stopped me and angrily asked me just where I thought I was going and just who I thought I was. I leaned toward her, raised my chin, grabbed my white, wrap-around, Pontiff III clerical collar and said, "Ever seen one of these?" I still cringe at my rudeness, but she stepped back and let me pass.

And yet I was there, in most cases, only as a pastor, not as a family member, certainly not the kind of family member who brings years of togetherness, of joys and sorrows shared, of common tasks small and great, all the things that let you sit with one another in easy silence.

Most of the time, it would be a while before you would be allowed in to see the person you came for, so you had to sit there a lot with the others. The less you knew the family, the harder it was. There were also times when I knew a family quite well and really had shared years with them, celebrated with them, and worked with them, but the people I knew weren't there. To make things worse, anyone in bad enough shape to require intensive care treatment needed something larger than our local hospital. Where I served, that meant certainly a fifty and possibly a hundred-fifty mile trip one way. The distance made it tough on everybody, as well as making it impossible to look in often through the day. Family members took turns on the waiting, I got there when I could get there and that was my time, so I often found myself sitting at length with second cousins I'd never met. I'm sure I made them more uncomfortable than they made me. I had to be there, but I couldn't help thinking they were probably hoping I wouldn't be there long.

I would often feel, much as I'd felt when I was an acolyte and first saw people distorted with violent grief, that I was violating a private scene, shamefully barging in on someone's nakedness. The less I knew them, the more visibly suffering they were, the more I felt like an intruder.

One of the worst long hospital stays I attended was of a young couple we had married a few years before, Scott and Caitlyn, both badly injured in a car crash, both taken to the surgical and critical care unit in one of the larger area hospitals. Scott had a serious head injury and wasn't being allowed to regain consciousness; Caitlyn was conscious but pretty beat up. They had two young children. My wife and I took turns going down to the hospital. We knew Scott's family very well; his mother was on the church council. We knew Caitlyn's family not at all. To give a further twist to the common misery, the families didn't get along that well. They were clearly from different social worlds. But both families, which were large, camped in the waiting room in large numbers, waiting for the precious times they would be allowed through the locked doors. When I entered the room, I felt both warm welcome and frosty suspicion and resentment. It was hard not to spend more and easier time with those I knew well, hard not to feel I was ignoring the others, no matter what I did: one more inevitable pastoral dilemma without solution.

(Every so often, these ghastly situations provided an unintended, unexpected, but pretty welcome moment of human comedy. One morning, in the parking lot, on my way in, I ran into two of Scott's brothers, out for a smoke. People are always glad to have some report they can give, if only because it gives them something to talk about. So they told me how the night had gone [not much happened] and how their brother was [no change]. In fact, though they could visit him, he was still unconscious. "Of course, you know," one said sagely, "Those nurses have been keeping him heavily seduced." I think it was the only morning I visited there that I began with a smile.)

The general sense in the waiting room was that Scott was the most seriously injured, that he might not survive or ever wake up, and that Caitlyn, though seriously injured, would almost certainly, in time, fully recover. You could sense the settled verdict of expectations when you walked in the room: one family tense, anxious; the other relaxed, hopeful. Then two things happened, almost at the same time: Scott showed signs of improvement, Caitlyn began complaining of more pain and discomfort. Everyone agreed she was looking worse. The emotional atmosphere in the room shifted: despair and hope traded places. It had to be terrible for Caitlyn's family, losing hope, to watch Scott's family gaining it, all of them trapped in the same waiting room.

Then one morning Caitlyn was dead. Something inside her had ruptured; apparently she had been awake and pointing to the area in pain, but none of the expensive machines had told enough of a story for the nurses to react to. Someone told me her doctor, when he saw her chart that morning, settled the coming lawsuit for good by bellowing for all to hear, "If you'd called me last night, she'd still be alive."

I thought the most bitter thing about this death was that Caitlyn's family was locked away from her in the next room and couldn't sit by her as she was dying. I remember thinking: if they're going to lock us out so they can watch closely and act quickly, then why didn't they? But it was like asking why we don't save everybody: one more pointless cry of protest that changes nothing.

I remember, when I was at seminary, there being a lot of agitation for courses that were practical: less systematic theology and more "what to say when you walk into a hospital room" or "how to talk to someone whose daughter died in the next room when she should have lived." We wanted something that would give us a script we could memorize, because we feared being alone with such things. But the grim truth is: there can be no such script. We have to create those moments on the spot.

A pastor who was my neighbor and mentor, Pastor Ken, as wise and canny as anyone I've ever met, told me once that the first thing you should do when you enter a hospital room is try not to say anything stupid. I guess it's like the old healer's code: first, do no harm. But he meant: pay attention to what's in front of you and don't diminish it. After that, I can only repeat what Christians have always said: trust in the spirit's guidance.

For all the rooms I sat in through all the years I served, I'm not sure I can remember a single thing I said.

V

Yet hovering around me, waiting within me, like a shadow thrown by who I was and why I was there, was the knowledge that, if death came, I would have to speak. The closer death was the more sharply I felt the life before me shaping itself toward the words I would speak after the gospel reading at the coming funeral, the meditation I would lead by my words for the family, for the community, for the church, on what we had, what we lost, who we were, and what we lived by.

I served in a Christian tradition that, more than some others, certainly more than the Roman Catholic church I grew up in, held the spoken word at the very center of its life, the source of faith, the clearest and least ambiguous bringer of the Word of God itself. But you don't need our theology or any theology at all to feel a summons to speech at the end of a life. We humans are the name-givers, the recorders and describers, the summarizers and meaning-seekers, of creation. At the times of greatest weight, the coming of the new or the passing of what we'll never see again, we want solemn gatherings and words of weight. We want to hear them and we want someone to speak them. Like the seed of ceremonies of farewell lying in our need to be present with each other, the seeds of final words and final blessings lie deep in our nature.

In one of my first salary discussions at the first parish my wife and I served, the council members were raising their eyebrows at the salary guidelines provided by the synod, wondering how they could reduce them to as little as possible, when one of them said, "It's just hard to put a price on something like this." It's the kind of expression of futility councils love and understand as an excuse to do as little as possible. Probably sensing this, the young council president leaned forward, scanned the faces, and tapped his pencil on the table for emphasis as he said, "Well, I'm going to tell you this: there's not enough money on this earth to get me to stand up in that pulpit and find something to say at a funeral the way we expect these people to do." They would all accept without question the necessity of speech at those times. And they knew as well, they knew in their bones, the seriousness they expected then and the difficulty of being the one called to provide it.

All the pastors where we served presided at a lot of funerals. As I noted earlier, that first parish was in a county that had the highest death rate in the state of Minnesota. The words we brought to funerals, like it or not, fair or not, were a great part of the way we were measured.

I read about one pastor who preached his own funeral sermon, recording it on video before his death. That at least seems to imply something about how he measured other pastors and himself. I'm guessing he meant it as (sort of) a voice from beyond the grave (though it wasn't really). I had a hard time shaking the picture of a church full of mourners staring at a tiny television set sitting atop the coffin. Weirdly, I wondered what he wore for the recording. (He reminded me of another pastor I read about in a history of the English Civil War who baptized himself. He couldn't find anyone else holy enough.)

But I've always thought it was an important part of church life and said something profound about the nature of the church that we had to speak for each other, from baptism to burial, just as we prayed for each other and blessed each other, that we had to yield ourselves into the hands and words of others.

When my mother died, my family scheduled the funeral before finding out when I could get there. We had just had an ice storm and the Grand Forks Airport, eighty miles away, had been closed. I got the first flight out after it opened Sunday afternoon. The roads getting there were solid ice. The funeral, in South Chicago, was the next morning. The airline lost my luggage, I walked into the wake at nine o'clock Sunday night, and they told me they'd arranged to have me preach.

I fully intended to refuse. I went to the rectory the next morning to do so but the priest presiding said he was just going to rattle aimlessly so I really should do it. Professionally, I was aghast at his remark, though, later, I concluded—perhaps generously—that he was trying to put me at ease. I did preach, but it was certainly not the sermon I would have wanted to give. More importantly, I felt seriously and essentially out of place doing it. I was not and had not been my mother's pastor. What I was and should have been allowed to be was a mourning son. Someone should have spoken for me and to me.

It's important that we speak for each other. The words are as creative as they are descriptive, even more so. They transcend us and raise us with them. They provide the bridge from the life that was to the life that will be, from what we lost to what we carry on with, what we carry on towards.

When I read the gospel at funeral services, had the congregation be seated, and looked out on those listening, I probably felt most strongly the privilege, the importance, the challenge, and the burden of the office I'd been called to.

VI

My friend Ken and I were coming back from a synod committee meeting one day. Ken was driving, because he couldn't tolerate anyone else's driving, and, for some reason, we were bringing the bishop with us. I was sitting in the back seat and the conversation had drifted to something we'd all been through: someone storming into your office to attack you for something you hadn't done, something you couldn't remember doing, something you thought you did pretty well, or, at any rate, something you were utterly shocked at being attacked for. The bishop was telling a story, which clearly still bothered him, of a furious man in his office the day after a funeral service, chewing him out for never once mentioning the deceased in his sermon.

The bishop said, "Well, I told him I hadn't really known the man, and he pounded his fist on my desk and said, 'You *knew* he was *sick*!'"

That image of wounded fury has stayed with me as a sign of how desperate we are, just then, in that final ritual, for some personal bond with the one we lost, some touch of the merely human. Then the bishop asked us, "Do you always talk about the person you're burying?"

Ken looked over his shoulder at me. We said, pretty neutrally, well, yes, we did, as far as we could, but that we almost always addressed the manner of death, the kind of loss, something about the life. (Ken and I shared such a close understanding of this that I can't really remember which of us said what.) The bishop, frowning thoughtfully, said, "Who told you to do that?"

Ken, eyes a bit wider, looked over his shoulder at me again. He had a little twitch he'd do with his head to express something like, "Can you believe what you're hearing?" He said, "It just seemed like a natural thing to do. And people respond to it, so . . . "

I rattled out something similar.

I'll have more to say below about how I shaped funeral sermons, but I did hear the issue of the place of the personal in funeral sermons discussed explicitly once. My homiletics instructor, Professor Tostengard, touched on it briefly when he addressed sermons for special occasions. He had said he had grown up hearing older pastors simply march through one biblical passage after another, as though nothing but the voice of God should be heard and mentioning human life would only mess things up. (I would hear a few of these myself.) He said he understood the ideal being practiced, allowing the saving Word to be all in all, and he didn't scorn it. "But I think," he said, smiling slyly, "I would consider that a trifle . . . austere," conveying clearly that he thought it was completely ridiculous and that only a benighted knucklehead would do it. At least that was what he conveyed to me. But his ideal for sermons in general was that they should have a strong human presence in them. He would often ask, especially after one of us delivered something too academic or abstract: "Where are your hearers in this sermon? And where are you?" So it was really natural for me to approach funeral sermons in the same way.

In our world, of course, the personal has a high value given to it already, and the challenge is not to let it swallow up everything else. You don't need to say that much to bring the person back to the congregation: the mourners do most of the work for you.

On an ordinary Sunday, the first part of the sermon has to be devoted to gathering the congregation into a kind of ideal listener, so you can take them together where you're going. At a funeral, this is already done for you by the loss and by the day. Everyone knows why they're there. You'll never have listeners who are more focused, who participate more, who bring more to your words, who enliven your presentation for themselves. You'll never experience more strongly the way a group creates an experience together.

Most people come to funerals wanting to believe everyone there knew and loved all those they loved and lost. They want to hear God loved them and loves them still. There's a flood of desire surging around you as you enter the pulpit: they want to believe your sermon is everything they could want it to be before you say a word.

Serving so long in the same isolated places, knowing many large families, I ended up going to lots of funerals in other churches. I squirmed once through a sermon I thought was distant and impersonal to the point of sounding almost generic. Yet after the service I was standing there when a family member told the pastor how good he thought the sermon was, and added, "You seemed to know him so well. He was just like that."

VII

And yet I worked hard to shape each sermon to the life we were gathering for. For our regular services, we follow a set lectionary that provides the scripture readings we use each Sunday. My ordinary preparation would begin with those and I'd be looking for things I didn't understand or things that stood out from the texts for some reason. I would hope the readings and the life around me would flow together (or fight together) as my mind turned them over through the week.

A funeral sermon, necessarily, reverses this process: it begins with one particular life which met one particular death. My first questions, those that set my direction, were thus: what kind of life was this and what kind of death?

I think, in most cases, it was the nature of the death that was before all of us most vividly. And the kind of death it was, peaceful or painful, sudden or drawn out, expected or not, come to infancy, to youth, to maturity, or to great age, shaped in great part the grief that we had. I almost always tried to characterize the kind of loss people were experiencing as a way of coming to where they were.

It's sometimes too easy and too tempting to make that your only question and then to soothe the loss with scriptural words of comfort and of promise. Tempting too is to see the loss as only a family loss, simply the loss of a loved one. Sometimes that really might be all that could be said, but not always. It was a particular life that ended, and I'd always consider the age, the character, the interests, and the work of the person, as far as I knew them or could find them out.

In the first town we served, I got to know the mayor fairly well, Mayor Vic, because he made sure he knew everyone that moved to town. It was through him that I met of lot of local authorities as well as some state legislators. Vic was a real character, too, roaming the town with stories and laughter, part of every group, every event, a tireless booster of the little our tiny village had. He belonged to the other church in town and, from the sermon at his funeral, you might not have known he was anything but a husband and a father and did anything but accept Jesus as his savior. I thought it was a missed opportunity to address the community's loss and celebrate the community's gifts. I suppose, to be fair, that sermon might have been the pastor's deliberate choice as the only important answer to who Vic was and to who any of us really were in the end. But I was always trying for more than that in the sermon.

And those were the things that shaped my choices of texts and hymns, so far as they were up to me: the kind of death, the kind of life. People will sometimes have favorite verses and often have favorite hymns. Too often, they tend to be things anyone might pick, e.g., Psalm 23, "Amazing Grace." But I was happy when they weren't because they gave me something to work with that I might not have thought of on my own. If I did get to choose, I would try to address both the particular grief and the particular life. For one awful, senseless death, I read as the gospel Jesus's cry of abandonment from the cross: "why have you forsaken me?" For another former mayor, I used the episode of the Roman centurion in Luke, the "man of authority," praised as a builder, who asks Jesus to heal his servant while declaring his own unworthiness.

We used the same general form for the readings as for the Sunday service—old testament reading, psalm, new testament reading, gospel—but by no means limited our choices to the standard passages that showed up in the handbooks or were printed in the hymnals. When my father died and was buried by the Roman Catholic parish I grew up in, I was quite surprised by how few choices I was given for both hymns and texts. (I was also surprised by how absent the parish priest was throughout the process. Our parish ideals and expectations had more of the personal in every sense.) It was another case of a narrow ideal dictating the shape of a rite that I thought could be enriched by allowing more force to the person at its center.

And if that person were less than beloved, not much of a spouse or parent, brought wreckage and little else to other lives, I thought that was something that still had to be faced. If you don't find some way to face the bitter realities of a life, you'll be the only one in the church that day not thinking about them. That doesn't mean I highlighted or bluntly proclaimed the ugliest truths about someone. For one thing, pastoral counseling over the years (and my own painful blunders) taught me that the worst things you've heard about a life are always more qualified, more complicated, than you think, even (and maybe especially) in the heart and mind of the wounded person telling you them. More importantly, we're speaking for Jesus, the friend of sinners, and commending this life to the God of mercy. But people should know you're as aware as they are of why mercy is needed.

I once attended the funeral of an extremely troubled man, someone at odds with much of the town, angry, bitter, even abusive. He'd sometimes approach people in the local diner to chastise them for their immoral behavior. He had a serious head wound from World War II, and most people saw that as the source of his trouble. But the pastor preaching the sermon set himself to do nothing but praise his Christian character. He read one of St. Paul's catalogs of Christian virtues, Galatians 5: 19–23. It begins with an enumeration of "works of the flesh" we are to spurn: obvious targets like fornication, impurity, licentiousness, as well as some interesting outliers like strife and factions. So the pastor began walking through the list, praising the man not only for avoiding drunkenness and carousing but also publicly condemning those vices in others, sometimes to their faces, as most of us were well aware. He skated a little over strife and anger, but fair enough: nobody's perfect, as most of us were also well aware. But then St. Paul continues, as the pastor had just reminded us by reading the passage, with the "fruit of the Spirit," a shorter list which included, glaringly, peace, patience, kindness, gentleness, and self-control.

St. Paul continued, but the pastor did not. He didn't say one word about Paul's sketch of the mild Christian character, not one, and everyone listening to him knew why. The silence roared in the church. The bottom dropped out of the sermon. Everything the pastor was saying sounded hollow, a false celebration of a Christian saint who didn't exist. He not only falsified the Christian ideal; he shut his eyes to the truth of a painful life. And he left no space for God's mercy.

I would say, in general, that the difference in approach to funerals between our tradition and some others was rooted deeply in our theological differences: we saw ourselves as commending a sinner to mercy; others, of which this pastor was a member, needed to see themselves as commending someone worthy to a well-earned reward. In death, as in life, the latter is a gilt-edged invitation to hypocrisy.

If I had been preaching at that funeral, I would not, for starters, use a passage of virtues like that. What was most evident about this man was how troubled he was, how driven to lash out at people and push them away. But another thing everyone in the church knew was that his family still loved him deeply and cared for him, often trying to make amends to people he hurt. It shouldn't be that hard to tell a story like that and open the way to a greater mercy.

But there are much harder cases, and those sermons are a misery to conceive, to compose, to deliver. You really can't know, in the charged atmosphere of funerals where there's been conflict or pain, what well-meant word is going to hurt or enrage somebody. After one of those, later in the day, I had to run an errand and stopped, on my way home, at a convenience store. The funeral had been for a man gone from his family for years, after what I gathered was a pretty rocky life together. The family, whom we knew well and liked a lot, had approached us because they had nowhere else to go. I was at the counter when I saw his daughter, who was about my age, walking toward me. It was one of those one-on-one encounters that, on a day like that, you'd just as soon not find yourself in. She stopped in from of me. "Those words today . . . ," she said. She put her hand on her chest, nodded. "Thank you."

That's the single moment I remember from that day, because I hadn't realized before then how very tied up in knots I'd been. I vividly recall how, when she spoke, I felt myself physically loosening, easing from within, as though my organs, my bones and nerves, my arms and legs, were releasing their twisted grip on each other and coming out right again because they'd been tapped by a magician's wand.

VIII

But as much as funerals are about remembering a person, they're also, brutally, about living on without that person. As much as I tried to bring a personal presence into the sermon, I saw the service itself as explicitly moving from the personal, out of the personal, into the future, into the hands of God. At the very end of the service, we leave the altar and stand at the coffin, declaring: "Into your hands, O merciful Savior, we commend your servant." Since the first words of our service were a proclamation of baptism, the funeral rite could be seen as an ideal, concentrated image of the Christian journey. It could also be understood as a Christian imperative: you must do this, you must go this way. It was our way of bringing the chaos of death, the varied mess of life and loss, into order, and I saw getting there as a spiritual struggle. I would sometimes have the sense, especially in shocking or agonizing losses, of almost physically wrestling people out of darkness, through ever narrowing corridors of decision; when the procession finally stepped out with the entrance hymn at the service, it was like sliding out at last into some kind of light.

An important stage of that wrestling was meeting with the family, ostensibly to plan for the funeral: pick the hymns and the readings, settle the details, and deal with any special concerns. But the deeper reason was to begin bringing order to death, to give shape to this turning point.

The meeting served, too, to sharpen and enliven our sense of the life we lost. Attending a death can be a very narrowing, entrapping experience: sharing stories gives back a breadth and freedom to the lives of the mourners. And it helped me know the person we were burying that much better. Even though we were at the same parishes for many years, even though we knew people well, we would still only know them in a limited way. (In a sense, this is true of everyone, and one of the gifts of funerals is that we can sometimes see a richness and variety in a life beyond what we know. I've seen adult children stunned by meeting friends and colleagues of their parents who had a much different view of them.)

This meeting was even more important when the person we were burying and, even worse, those planning the funeral were completely unknown to us. In those cases, we sometimes had to insist on meeting them: they couldn't understand why we couldn't just mumble a few prayers and call it a day. But it was in just those cases that some contact was necessary, first, to take the edge off the suspicion or at least the discomfort they might feel about the church. And there was no other way to get some sense both of their grief and of the person being buried.

We did a funeral for a man who'd been gone from our town for years, who had lived roughly and died young. His only surviving relative was his sister, who'd also been gone for years. She had to fly in from California and she brought a friend who claimed to be a kind of free-lance minister. (In my experience, friends with spiritual interests and out-of-town relatives who are active members of fundamentalist churches provide the greatest challenges in meetings like this.) They, especially the friend, couldn't understand why we had to use our standard funeral rite, complete with the Apostles' Creed and the Lord's Prayer, why we had to process and recess a certain way and have a set of scripture readings, why they couldn't design their own service from the ground up. Late in this discussion, the friend burst out, "I lead funerals and weddings all the time and every single one of them is completely different." My memory draws a merciful veil over my reply, but on this we never compromised. As we saw it, the funeral rite was the last defining moment of a spiritual journey and, in the church we served, it simply had to be the way it was.

But there's a greater point to be made here which, in these days of novelty, can't be made too often: the power of a rite depends on the repetition of that rite. Asking a group to join in the Lord's Prayer, likely to be known well to them, is to summon a spiritual order into being, and you can feel it forming around you; the Rosary, for Roman Catholics, would have a similar, or greater force; the funeral rite, with its set proclamations and prayers, its set choreography, its involvement of the congregation, offers the same power. At the same time, the elements unique to each funeral—hymns, lessons, the sermon—gain in power by standing out from a familiar form. Also, the way the funeral rite closely follows our ordinary Sunday service joins the funeral gathering to the greater life of the church. My wife and I certainly didn't see ourselves as free-lance ministers, eager to be hired for special occasions. We were pastors of a congregation which itself was a member of a particular Christian tradition. We presided at funerals because we first presided at the worship of the parish. Part of our task in worship, including at funerals, was to speak for the community we served, in the greatest sense: this congregation, the Lutheran tradition, the Christian church, the communion of saints.

As with many things in parish ministry, you may feel like you're the only one in the church that believes that but you have to act out of that belief anyway. My hope was that people who had grown up in the tradition might have an instinctive grasp of such things. We usually didn't have to argue explicitly about the service and, when we did, people from the church council usually backed us up. But, as I've said, in our time the urge to personalize everything is strong and, in a time of grief, can be pretty demanding. It's too easy for families to think their loss is the only loss and that the funeral belongs to them.

If family members wanted to speak or to give readings of their own, I always wanted to place these early in the service. I liked to have any solo performances of music early, too, preferably before the sermon. For one thing, I think it's easier on the person doing it—sometimes unwillingly—to get it over with early. The pressure in a funeral mounts as it nears the end. Anyone who thinks it would be touching to have a young person sing just before the coffin is wheeled out shouldn't be indulged, or should have to sing themselves. But, more deeply, I wanted to preserve the essential movement of the rite, out of the personal, into God's hands.

One of the hardest discussions we had on this issue was at the funeral for a young man, a very talented actor and singer, with a beautiful voice, who'd grown up in the congregation. He'd been in our daughter's class in junior high and high school, so we knew him quite well. We planned the funeral on one of his last days, before they took him off life support. He knew a lot about music and made excellent selections; the college choir he'd been part of only a few years earlier was going to provide the non-congregational music. I thought things were settled. But, after his death and a day or so before the funeral, someone in the family had an idea: they had several recordings of the young man singing and they wanted to fill the funeral with his voice; most particularly, they wanted to hear him singing at the very end, as his coffin moved down the aisle. (Because of how young he was, how well known and loved, we'd had to move the funeral to the largest church in town, and it was a long aisle.)

Mary Carol, who would be preaching, and I were stunned. Rightly or wrongly, we thought hearing that beautiful, lost voice, singing alone, at that heaviest of moments would be devastating. Any transcendence the service had managed to reach would be shattered. Ordinarily, at that moment, the congregation is singing, and, if it's been up to me, they're singing something they know really well. It's still moving, because of when it's happening; the worse the death, the more miserable that moment is; but all those voices around you singing together radiate strength and bear you up. We liked these people, it would be easy to let them have their way, but in our judgment, rightly or wrongly, it would be an awful thing to do to everybody and would betray what the service ought to be.

It was a painful discussion, but we did talk them out of it. We had the recordings played in the church before the service as a prelude, up to the moment we would begin the service at the back with our usual baptismal declaration, then process in.

As we gathered the procession, listening to the young man sing, the grief descending on everyone was crushing. I think, at that moment, I'd never been more sure that we were right about a decision we'd struggled with. I was choking on sorrow myself and could barely get my first lines out. Hardly anyone could get through their readings without breaking down. During the choir pieces, members of the choir would sink down sobbing into their pews, then rally and rise as others dropped out. When we recessed, walking with the coffin down that long aisle, the voices of the congregation singing around us, it really was a powerful, almost literally uplifting moment. I couldn't imagine having to take that walk with only the young man's voice over us. I told the funeral director if we'd given in to the family the funeral would have been pointless: we might all just as well have sobbed for an hour, then crawled home.

IX

One not uncommon request we received, especially in the first area we served, was to have another pastor, sometimes a relative but usually someone local, involved in the service, usually by providing what amounted to another sermon. I was never sure what was behind these requests. They usually didn't come from our regular members so my guess was it might have been a way to bring a comfortable presence into an uncomfortable situation. (On the very rare occasions the request did come from a family I had known long and known well, I took it as another opportunity to reflect on how little I understood human beings.) Families would always say the pastor was a personal friend but, as often as not, there was little that was personal in what they said. We would usually be treated to a tour of the Bible and a reminder that there was no better day to accept Jesus into our own hearts. One cynic observed that the more worried families were about someone's life and character, the more pastors would be asked to be in the funeral.

There was a retired pastor in the area who'd had a radio show during his time of service so he was often asked to speak at funerals as a kind of celebrity orator. He was a quiet, courtly man who greatly resembled the aged Karl Barth. He had a thick, charming Norwegian accent, always said he was "asked to bring a greeting," spoke briefly, and fit smoothly and graciously into the service. As the years went on, I could almost see him as one of our regular assisting ministers; he would grasp my hand before the service, nod, and say, in his choppy English, "We have done this together before."

The hardest times were those in which the request came out of some animosity: a struggle in the family, a struggle with the church, a problem someone had with me or with my wife. (The pastor I discussed earlier, who could only bring himself to address half of a Pauline passage on virtue, was specifically requested by the deceased as a rebuke to the regular pastor of his church.) In one case, a family demanded the guest pastor deliver the main sermon, and we got a hint they would just as soon have him do the entire funeral, with us staying home. Most of our church councils had at least a few veterans of small-town squabbles and, in this case, had enough experience of that family to refuse even to consider such a thing. I seem to remember one elder slapping his hand on the table and barking, "Absolutely not," though that may be wishful thinking (or remembering). I do remember telling the family that, as a pastor of the church, I didn't have to speak at length but I did have the responsibility to speak. One of the men, looking at the floor, nodded and said he guessed he really couldn't tell me I couldn't say anything. But, after the funeral, they joined a church in another town.

At the second parish we served, one younger pastor, who'd grown up in the area but didn't seem to be attached to any church, was always appearing in different churches as a guest preacher for funerals. Someone finally told me he was actively lobbying families to be in them. He actually peeked into the vestry just before one of our funerals, as we were putting on our vestments, said, "Just let me know when you want me to come up," and sauntered back to his pew. Mary Carol and I stared at each other. We hadn't heard anything about this, so we went looking for the family members we'd planned the funeral with. They hadn't heard anything about it either. One indignant woman said, "That man has no business speaking at our funeral. Don't you call him up." I noticed him during the service, ready to pop up when anything ended. After the service, he just strolled away, no doubt hoping for better luck some other time.

Our usual procedure, in all these cases, was to treat guest preachers as another personal element in the service and to have them speak near the beginning. Thus, by the time of the gospel reading, followed by the sermon one of us would deliver, the service was taking on the shape it normally had.

Since my wife and I served together, we sometimes got a request that one of us would speak rather than the other. We would each, inevitably, know some people and some families better than others. In those cases, the decision would be natural. The difficulty, again, would be if the request were coming out of some animosity. Also, we served in fairly remote places which hadn't seen many women pastors, and there were people who still didn't regard them as real pastors, an attitude we simply could not encourage. And in this matter, too, the moral weight of loss and the sense that funerals belong to the bereaved brought their own force.

In general, we tried to keep preaching assignments as our decision. Staff ministries always provide lots of opportunities for jealousy and rivalry, and allowing them to develop and fester will poison a congregation. Before we were even ordained and had any idea we'd be serving together, one senior pastor, whose assistants revered him, told us he never wanted his congregation to know who was preaching on any given Sunday, so they couldn't choose which preacher they wanted to hear. He said, "You can't stop people from liking one of you more than the other. But you can keep from encouraging it. Never help split your own congregation." Sage advice, we always thought, and we tried to extend the same principle to funerals. But it is one more time when concerns which trouble a pastor's decisions can seem petty and insensitive to everyone else.

Towards the end of our service, we were set to do the funeral of a sister of one of our regular members, an elderly widow who usually had the council presidents tearing their hair out. No issue was too small for Katherine's attention; no reasons had any weight that weren't hers. A couple of days before the funeral, the funeral director called on the phone. "Pastor," he said, "I got a . . . request from Katherine."

I thought I could hear his amusement threatening to overcome him. "Let's hear it."

"Well, it's a bit more than a request. Katherine says your wife has to preach at her sister's funeral."

"Ah. Because—?"

"She says she's been listening to you for ten years and she hasn't understood one word you've said."

We told Katherine stories. Joe, the funeral director, told me some of her other requests, from the quaint to the impossible.

In this case, it wasn't hard to let Katherine have her way.

X

We were blessed, throughout our service, with excellent funeral directors, skilled and compassionate people who made painful but necessary decisions easier to settle and who made our tasks easier by their competence and reliability. We bonded quickly with all of them and our pretty frictionless teamwork spared everybody a lot of trouble.

There was often a little prayer service for family and close friends the evening before the funeral, during the wake at the funeral home. Usually, either my wife or I would do this alone, depending on which of us wasn't preaching at the funeral itself. It's not the kind of event you could just walk in and out of, so, when it was my turn, I'd spend a while there, usually talking shop with whichever funeral director was on duty.

One afternoon, I somehow ended up talking about sermons with Henry, elder brother of the family who owned the home. I'm not sure how we got there or what we discussed: what I remember was a story Henry told about a student pastor in his intern year, doing his first funeral. He showed up at the funeral home a day or so before the funeral, extremely nervous: his supervising pastor was out of town, and Henry got the impression he hadn't attended that many funerals in his own life. The young man wanted Henry to tell him what to say in the sermon. Henry told him, "Well, that has to come out of your heart." Henry said he left looking as though he were heading for his own death and probably wishing he was.

On the day of the funeral, the service was going along reasonably well, and it came time for the sermon. The young man stood in the pulpit, pale and trembling, wide-eyed, scanning the room. Then he threw out his arms, and shouted, "I HATE DEATH."

Clearly, he had let his heart speak, in all its terror. I sympathize with the terror.

I worked hard at those sermons, and I won't forget the agony and sweat, the sick stomach, the feeling of stepping through a minefield, not wanting to send people off into some tangled rage of their own. I learned early in my service, too, that all the work done to explore the life lost and the grief really guarantees nothing, and that you could be wrong about everything. I remember being convinced by one family about the peacefulness of the death and their serene acceptance of it and finding later I was wildly mistaken. I never lost the fear of making the same mistake again.

And yet, working at my desk gave me, in some ways, an oasis of peace within that time of death. I always liked being at my desk: I found the time for reflection and the solitude refreshing. This was especially valuable amid the intense human contacts of the days surrounding a funeral. I wrote out my sermons by hand. My handwriting—actually, my printing, for the sake of legibility—made the manuscript a friendlier, more recognizable presence, and it became for me a kind of talisman to carry to the service. Standing in the pulpit, especially at a large funeral or a particularly wrenching death, can be a lonely experience. Those worked-over sheets of paper bearing my own marks were nice to have in front of me.

By the time I got to my desk, all the planning and all the arrangements were usually finished. This helped protect my time and give purity to my focus. I liked to have some say in the choice of hymns and texts, especially texts, so they had some resonance with this death, these mourners. If I hadn't, I would still search for ways that the family's choices bore on the death and the life before us. The agony and sweat also flowed powerfully from what I was called to achieve in the proclamation: expressing the nature of *this* death, the spiritual place of *these* mourners, where the Christian call and the Christian promise came *here*.

If possible, I liked to have an entire day set aside for my writing, so there wouldn't be a break in the composition. It would usually take me about five or six hours to shape and to write out a funeral sermon, assuming I had a rough outline when I started. I liked to start in the morning and finish by late afternoon. If I couldn't, that usually meant I was too tired to think, but that's a reality in parish ministry and things have to be done anyway. But, at all costs, I needed to wake on the day of the funeral with the sermon done. Just being done gave me peace.

I never completely relaxed until the service, the graveside service, the lunch, and the final conversations were over, but having the physical reality of those filled pages was enough to calm me and keep most of my anxieties under control.

XI

Once people started gathering, at the wake and at the church before the service, you could see life becoming livelier again. People find their way through even the most painful loss by coming together, touching each other, telling stories, literally bringing memories to life. The effort people make to dress up for each other out of love and respect, when crushed by grief, always seemed to me a moving act of human defiance before an unwanted reality. Towards the end of our parish service, slide shows of photographs and elaborate memory tables became more and more common; adding that visual dimension to the storytelling was a great gift.

I think both the photographs and the gathering itself drew on something deeper which I touched on earlier: how important vision is to us, wanting and needing to see each other.

One of the things I came to appreciate and to value was the formal viewing of the restored bodies of the dead. When I first saw the dead, set formally and finely clothed in their coffins, I wasn't sure what I thought. The lifeless stillness of someone you know and might have spoken to recently is strange, uncanny, and the strangeness never really goes away. Then, just before the service, seeing the coffin closed over that familiar body can be like seeing a life crushed out in front of you; the funeral directors usually had us in another room, praying with the family, when they did this.

But I saw, over the years, how much seeing again the person they lost could mean to people. This was especially true when someone had died slowly and painfully, wasting away until they were unrecognizable, or even when someone had been homebound, long severed from common life. Seeing someone again, at peace now, was like a last embrace. We buried a woman, not that old, who had dwindled, from cancer, to almost nothing. The funeral director made her look vibrant again, and her two daughters dressed her in bright red, the most outlandish outfit she owned. I had watched her waste away. Now she looked beautiful and you could see the joy in her daughters as they smiled down at her.

And it could be devastating when people didn't get that sight. We knew two elderly brothers who both had great difficulty getting about. They hadn't seen each other for a long time when one of them suddenly died and a nephew who was handling his affairs had him cremated immediately. I don't think his brother ever recovered from being denied a last look, ever got over his anger at the nephew or his own failure to reach out before the end.

Cremations became more common through the years, but I still thought it was important to have a formal viewing and have a coffin set before the altar at the funeral; there was no reason the cremation couldn't come after the service. The coffin's an eerie presence, but an important one, and the gestures of blessing, the nearness of the Paschal candle, shining with Easter's light, and the gathering and processing of mourners lose some of their force without it.

At the very least, the urn ought to be at the service to provide a focus. Still, an urn on a table or someone carrying an urn never matched for me a coffin's presence near the mourners in the pews or a coffin being carried to an open grave by pallbearers. But customs surrounding death are inevitably rooted in your own experience and tradition and the emotions surrounding them aren't always shared.

One of the worst funerals we did was for a young girl who'd been a confirmation student of ours. She got in some minor trouble but was sent, a bit unfairly, most of us thought, to a juvenile home. There she met a wilder girl and they ran away together. She was cut in half by a train as they were racing across the tracks. Mary Carol took the call in the middle of the night and had to accompany a sheriff's deputy to tell her mother. They needed the mother's permission to get dental records so they could identify the body.

There was no question of her body being viewed. But here's how strong the need to see is:

Two days before the service, the funeral director, Tom, called us. He wanted us to come to the funeral home: the girl's mother, Betty, was there, demanding to see her daughter; Tom wanted us to help him talk her out of it.

Tom was the first funeral director we worked with, and we probably did most of our funerals with him. Easy to work with, compassionate, he was treasured by the community and had been at his funeral home longer than most area pastors had served their churches. He was also the county coroner and had often remarked to me how gruesome it was to pick up shattered bodies from car wrecks. He'd say, "I wish I could make these young drivers see what I have to see." But he was facing a mother who wanted that sight, and he would do everything he could to stop her.

At the time, I thought of Tom as protecting the mother because he was a sensitive person and much of his profession involved blunting the force of death. Looking back now, it's hard not to also see him as one more man drawing a boundary for a woman.

But my wife and I instinctively sided with the mother. We thought all parents had the right, if not the duty, to see what had come upon their child. So we went, knowing we surprised Tom, knowing we were putting him in a corner.

At the reception area in the funeral home, we restated our support of Betty. Tom made his case again, about the poor condition of the body, how it was probably beyond recognition, pointing out it had taken dental records to identify. By this time, Betty was so fiercely resolved to see what was left of her daughter that I don't think she'd have given in even if we had supported Tom. So he nodded, then said he wanted us to see the body first.

I think he thought, if we saw what he had to see, we really would see differently and tell Betty she had to let it go. But we were probably as bullheaded as the young drivers he wished he could enlighten.

He led us into the back. There was a body bag on a table. He unzipped the bag and spread it open. The girl was in pieces. He picked up her arm. "Look." He lifted a thick flap of skin on the side of her face to show us how little was left of her head.

He told us there just wasn't much he could do to keep the body together and provide a viewing. I don't know how exactly I imagined Betty would look at the body; I don't remember even trying to picture it. But we still thought he had to give her something.

And he did. As opposed as he was, once he saw we wouldn't give in, he considered things settled. He would do what he could and asked us to sit with Betty until he was ready. He was more gracious than I probably would have been.

He came out after a few moments and explained to Betty what she would see: the body under a covering, with only her face exposed, surrounded by a white cloth.

We entered the viewing room, Tom leading us, my wife and I on either side of Betty. We saw just what Tom said we would. I thought I might have been looking at any child's face.

But Tom had given Betty what she needed. She sagged back against us. I don't think I'll ever forget the pressure of her body falling against mine. She moaned and spoke, but not to us: she spoke to the daughter she was finally seeing again: "Oh. Look at you."

Then we all went home, with whatever peace you could have with a loss that could never be made good.

XII

Years later, I was speaking with another mother whose child had been killed. She was a member of our congregation and sang in our small choir, as Mary Carol and I both did, so we knew her pretty well. She also had a little beauty shop where she gave low-priced haircuts, making her a favorite of the local men, and I spent a lot of hours, over the years, chatting with her, inevitably about family life. Her daughter had died in a car collision, long before we had come to the congregation.

One day, something had brought her daughter's death back to her. I was never clear how this happened, but somehow she and her husband both arrived at the scene, he a little before her. She said her only thought was to get to the car, to reach her child, so she drove as close as she could, then ran from her vehicle. Her husband grabbed her, lifted her up, and carried her away, told her she couldn't look.

I interrupted her, because I was so certain the point of her story was that she got loose, that no one was able to prevent her from seeing her daughter. I groaned and stated my principle, assuming I was affirming her, "Parents have the right to see anything that's happened to their kids. People always think they're protecting you."

She stopped clipping and looked at me wide-eyed. "Oh, no. He was right. I'm glad he stopped me."

It was one of those jolting reminders I received on a regular basis: no matter how clearly valuable I thought something was, not everyone was going to agree with me. There were people who wouldn't look at open coffins; there were people who left instructions their bodies were not to be viewed.

To see, to turn from; to be seen, to hide; to cling together, to be alone. So much that's so deep in us, our needs, our desires, can be at war within us and among us. There would always be someone, painfully, left out, repelled, by what everyone else wanted. There would always be a lot of us, when death came, who didn't know what we wanted or what we would regret.

XIII

I often found it reassuring, especially if I'd struggled with a sermon, that my words weren't the only words spoken the day of the burial. In our tradition, the sermon is set firmly within the funeral rite. If I could choose the hymn that followed the sermon, then that hymn could often serve as the sermon's ending, or at least a carrying of my words into a broader vision. But, more importantly, the words of the day would flow from centuries of Christian meditation: the hymns and passages of scripture chosen for the service, and, most importantly, the creed, the set prayers, and the form of the service itself. The worship leaders weren't alone at the front of the church, and the mourners weren't there as strangers: the communion of saints was speaking around us and through us.

Like many aspects of worship, this wasn't something I expected everyone to be able to articulate or even be very conscious of. My faith was that nevertheless it would bring its power to them, its gift of community. But sometimes people could be surprisingly aware of just that reality of communion the service offered.

After one service, we had returned from the cemetery, and I was making my way around the assembly hall during the funeral lunch when a man I didn't know came up to me. "I wanted to thank you for the service," he said, "And tell you how much I appreciated it." Then he added, "I mean the service, not the sermon. I thought the sermon was fine, but it was your service that really impressed me. I go to a lot of funerals in these communities and most of them make me feel like an outsider. They treat me as though I didn't have any faith and still need to be called to Jesus. But I come to them as a person of faith, and your service clearly assumed I was, that I was here—or we were here together—lifting up one of us to God's care. So thanks."

Memory has no doubt polished that comment (since my visitor sounds so much like me); I've fondled it for over twenty years. It was pretty rare to encounter that level of perception. But it was nice to hear, and I knew what he meant about the area's churches. Most of them would describe themselves as free or independent or gospel centered or spirit led or Bible believing, but they tended to share one fairly narrow theological take on Christian life and experience, orbiting around a conscious decision of faith, adult baptism, a personal conversion narrative, and a life of explicit holiness. It was necessary for them to assert the faith and holiness of the departed and to challenge the mourners to accept the same faith, indeed, to assume they haven't yet. These aren't necessarily bad things, but they're not the only things in the Christian life, nor do they describe the only way to live it. To Lutheran ears, they leave out the very things that loom large for us at funerals: the gift of faith, the baptism of infants within a community, the reality of sin and struggle in the best of lives, the mercy of God beyond all our deserving, the reality of grace in the worst of lives.

This leads to a greater point that transcends church divisions: our service was shaped by our theology but, beyond that, it was bound to our way of life as Christians. I remember reading in the memoirs of stage and film director Tony Richardson how uncomfortable he grew with show business funerals. He was going to a lot of them in the years when AIDS was first bringing its devastation; I remember him saying he simply stopped attending funerals because no one seemed to know what to do at them. This may be a faulty memory but I recall the sense of someone who couldn't assimilate death, so many deaths, into the life he lived, the ways of his community. I would certainly never claim that death is easy for Christians to accept, and I hope these pages have already confirmed that. But death is part of the Christian's lifelong meditation. As unwanted, shocking, and unacceptable as it might be, as horrible the manner in which it might come, death is always part of the life a Christian lives. We know what to say and do at funerals because we've been saying and doing the same or similar things all our lives.

In the parishes we served, most funerals were parish events. Those who filled the pews were usually a good share of those who filled the pews on Sunday. Also, in our small communities, we had regulars from outside the congregation who would attend the funerals of anyone from town. Because we would, in any case, see the service as a parish event, we would both normally lead the service. Save for the presence of the coffin and the address in the sermon of one particular death, you might have thought you were at one more Sunday celebration.

There is power in that, a force for steadfastness, a force for strength and communion, a force carried by the ritual gathering, both the ritual itself and the random human gathering, made one by the ritual. The power was certainly there for me, especially with the bad ones, especially when there was simply no consolation, and especially if I'd struggled with the sermon and felt I'd lost, all those words from other people, other times, other voices around me, lifted me up and set me again within what we'd always done as a worshipping people. It was nice to know, and to feel, that I wasn't the only one talking.

XIV

Finally, all the words will be said. Most often, we would end at the grave, to face bluntly its reality and finality: earth to earth, ashes to ashes, dust to dust. We stood around the gaping earth, with the coffin held above it until its lowering, and we were no longer defining one life but proclaiming an alternate reality. It was like arguing with someone who only stares back at you in silence, impassively, unwaveringly, until the meaning of your own speech seems to dissolve.

We creatures of earth have been speaking about death since we began speaking; we've been constructing beliefs about life and death since we began thinking. Many words, different beliefs, but the end never changes: the earth, the fire, the wind, the sea, the elements that never change, receive what's left of us, no matter what we say or believe.

There's a concentration and focus to the funeral experience that increases and intensifies through the service itself and the journey to the cemetery. But disorder is always tugging at it, unraveling the order we're weaving as we're weaving it. The sorrow, the loss, the empty future days, drag us away to the shadows: they're powerful precisely because they're not distractions; they're reminders of the bitter dimensions of why we're doing what we're doing.

I could feel, during the service, as I was delivering the sermon, that I was engaged in something of value, defining one person's life, like polishing a jewel, defining the Christian vision and way, something of power to stand before decay and corruption. But I could feel, too, how small my words were, spoken within a cacophony of others, all spoken within a vast, cold universe whose forces didn't care what we said or thought, and there was no way to know what good any of it did.

All of us are going to stop talking, and the silence of the grave will still be there. Its chilling threat isn't that it's saying something else: it's that it's not saying anything at all.

PART THREE

For All the Saints

I

I wanted to present, at this point, some of the sermons I gave during my service, both as a filling out of the story I've been telling and as examples of my most explicitly worked out meditations on the coming of death. I chose two that came out of episodes I discussed: Kay, the elderly woman I sat with as she died (Introduction), and Caitlyn, the young woman in the car crash who shouldn't have died (Part Two, Section IV). Two more are those I alluded to when I discussed shaping the sermon to the life (Part Two, Section VII): one for a retired mayor, the other for a man estranged from his family. I added two more, to illustrate the challenging and the typical: one for a man who took his own life, the other for a beloved and respected man, who died peacefully.

I'll list the readings that were used in each service before the sermon. They were chosen to speak to the life and death we were gathered for that day and they provided the immediate context out of which the sermon was proclaimed. Readers should take the trouble to look them up before proceeding to the sermon.

II. KAY

The readings for the service were:
Ecclesiastes 3: 1–14; Psalm 23; I Corinthians 12: 31—13: 13; Luke 2: 25–32.
Faith Lutheran, Eagle Bend, MN
October 5, 2002

Kay's life was long and rich, and her death was peaceful. Traditional readings like Ecclesiastes 3 and Psalm 23 were especially appropriate: Ecclesiastes for its broad vision of time, Psalm 23 for its serenity. I chose, from Luke's gospel, Simeon's cry of fulfillment when he embraces the Christ child in the temple. Lutherans of my generation would have been familiar with his song, the *Nunc Dimittis*, usually sung as the post-communion canticle in our Sunday service. One of our older members, at the funeral, told me she was outraged more people hadn't attended, given how involved Kay had been in the community. I thought she was being a little unfair, given that Kay had outlived most of her contemporaries, but I decided she was probably just expressing how great a presence Kay was in her life.

We enter *our* place of worship today, and we bring before God one of *our* old ones: a woman who also was righteous and devout, waiting for her consolation, with the touch of the Spirit on her. And these words of departure are fit to grace this servant of the Lord, one of the living stones of Christ's temple: they testify to the fullness of a life, the faithfulness of a life; they yield in peace to its passing; they rest on the hope of God's glory.

Kay knew that peace and hope, and not just as something to turn to at the end: she lived within it, as a kind of atmosphere of the spirit. She could have spoken words like this for some time now, out of a length of days, purely as a declaration of peace; we would have declared her life no less faithful and no less full. But, these last days, it has clearly been the time of departure, and this became the prayer for her: Lord, now let your servant go in peace. And so she did.

We carry *her* today, with that human reverence and love for those who've touched our lives. But who does not think of Kay as the one who did the carrying, with someone in her arms, caring for little ones, caring for older ones, and praising God? We praise God, too, and thank God for her.

The first time I saw her I thought of a happy elf or a leprechaun; she had grey hair and wrinkles, but there was something youthful in her, fresh, that eagerness we see in children, joyous, I guess: twinkling eyes, dimpled smile, a slight and fetching lisp in a melodious voice. She seemed to have a natural, instinctive welcome; when you came upon her, her look wasn't "Now who's this?" but "Whoever you are, welcome." You felt a radiance of goodness and joy.

Over the last couple of years, her conversations doubled back a little on themselves, then they got a little shorter, then came down, mostly, to the look and touch of bare presence. But the smile rarely failed. And she would always say, nodding her round head, "So nice to see you. Thank you for coming."

We can celebrate her life with thanksgiving and joy, and we can be at peace at her end. Just last summer, the family gathered for her hundredth birthday. One hundred years. She lived more years and more ably than most of us dare to hope for. She lived from one age to another, across a century of so many changes that our time, our ways, our very land, would be almost unrecognizable to those who saw her birth.

We know Ecclesiastes only tells the sober truth when it declares the first times of our life to be the time to be born and the time to die: those are our limits, whatever else we find time for, and the one comes with the other. But Kay certainly pushed the limit.

And though we think of the last century as a time of change, a time of wild extremes, Kay presents us with a concentrated life, of great continuity; what she was, she always was: one of the healers, those who build up, one of those there to embrace.

She grew up in a time when people needed the helping hands of family and friends, because there weren't a lot of other hands out there. Kay Nuland provided those hands.

We hearken so readily to the words of Psalm 23 because it calls us to find in God what we treasure in each other; we learn the satisfaction of love, the ways of love, and the hope for eternal love from those who care for us. Not just the comfort and the spread table: but the spirit that fills them and surrounds them, the spirit that revives our soul, the comforting presence in the dark times.

Kay was a mother without being a mother, a second mother to many—and not just those in her family. Many of the children who came through our Sunday school classes or Bible schools kept her in their lives, including and embracing her at their weddings, because she had embraced them.

It seemed to be, for her, a decision for life, a life direction settled early, a calling, a high vocation: to be a helper, a caretaker, for those who needed one.

If you recited the bare details of her life, without knowing her, they might seem like a recipe for a narrow, constricted life, one that had missed out on a lot: hardly budging from local scenes, not marrying, staying home to care for her parents, the younger children, denying herself, always seeming to be thwarted by circumstances when she tried to continue her schooling.

But to meet Kay was to meet someone with riches within her. What to others would be deprivations, to her *were* as parts of a calling. She *made good* her time—and, with all she did, still managed to become skilled enough as a nurse to be in charge of a surgical floor. She made good her time: found goodness in it, filled it with her goodness.

The famous passage on love from Paul's letter to the Corinthians is one we often hear at weddings: but it's really meant for all Christians, for all times, the greater gifts the Christian should strive for, the more excellent way, the Christian's true path.

"If I speak in the tongues of mortals and of angels, if I can move mountains, if I give away all my possessions, but have not love, I am a noisy gong, I am nothing, I gain nothing."

"Love is patient; love is kind . . . it doesn't insist on its own way . . . It bears all things . . . hopes all things, endures all things." Saying Paul's words at Kay's passing, we see her face.

We're all called to walk that way, though we don't always manage it. But beneath the world's noise, far from fame, in each Christian community, we treasure those who show that way. If they weren't among us, the spirit would go out of us entirely.

And when Pastor Mary Carol and I came here a few years ago, and started to learn who was who, and who were the ones who might not be active now but were once a part of the place, people would talk about "Kay Nuland" the way they might talk about "Abe Lincoln," or "Florence Nightingale," or "Mother Teresa." Her very name was like a title. In fact, somebody said flat out, the other day: "She was our Mother Teresa." She was a legend. Somebody else said: when she was here, she was the life and soul of the place. There are a lot of witnesses here to Kay's witness.

And that way of the Christian is meant to lead us beyond ourselves, to uncover what it is in us that will last, what it is that has eternal weight, what will take us to eternity.

Paul was setting out something beyond the marks of Christian conduct. He was meditating on human greatness, what is worthy in life as such: not the momentous, not the spectacular, but the way of love. Love never ends; it's the Christian way because it is the way of God, the way to the heart of God. This, of all we do and are, will last.

We commend Kay to that love today, with sure confidence. She cannot fail to find the end of the path she travelled on so steadily.

Let me borrow her words and say: "Kay, it was so nice to see you. Thank you for coming among us."

Now may the Good Shepherd embrace her with goodness and mercy, and may she dwell with the Lord forever. And may the Lord's goodness and mercy descend on us and abide with us. As we yield the loved one we must, may God grant us peace with her, and let us rest on the hope, as Kay rests in the presence, of the love that never ends.

Amen.

III. CAITLYN

The readings for the service were:
Isaiah 43: 1–3a; Psalm 23; Romans 14: 5b–9; Matthew 26: 36–39.
Zion Lutheran, Lake Bronson, MN
September 25, 1996

I told Caitlyn's story earlier: how she, her husband Scott, and her children were injured in a car crash; how long the intensive care vigil was; how hope turned to despair; how swift her death was. As of the day of her burial, Scott was still unconscious, and no one knew what shape he would be in when he was allowed to wake. Psalm 23 was here for its explicit proclamation of God's presence at the extremity of life, as were Isaiah and Romans. Jesus's very human trembling at the approach of his own violent end seemed to speak more strongly that day than any of his soothing promises. My one visual memory of the service was of stepping into the pulpit and looking out on faces that still seemed frozen in shock.

Jesus bows finally to what must be, as we all must, but it's his human cry to be spared, his sick sorrow at the approach of death, that brings him so close to us. He is already within the shadow of his suffering, and all that attaches him to our life here wants to flee, wants to pull even against his divine purpose. He's in a storm of emotion and desperation. "If it is possible, my father, let this cup of pain be taken away."

He prays, as we pray, because there is nothing else he can do, and the world he loves has no help in it. So he puts his sorrow and his faith together and simply holds them up to the mystery of God, in naked honesty, because God is all there is to appeal to and only God can sort them out.

But he still wants his friends near him when he prays. His asking them to stay and watch with him is as heartfelt and as eloquent of the mystery of Jesus as his wanting the cup to pass or his final "Your will be done." He wants them there not for what they can do but for who they are: they've shared his life; they're his close bond to the world he loves. They bring their own mystery: the helpless beauty and warmth of human presence.

We too bring ourselves together here, in that human mystery, as we have been watching and waiting together for days, clinging close: like children before something they don't understand—and we don't understand. We too pray because there is nothing else we can do, and we have been praying—we here, and many others. We wanted this cup to pass from us.

We give Caitlyn to God today, in prayer, and out of our storm of emotion and desperation. We send her to God adorned with our love, the deepest gift of earth and of human hearts. And our love and our prayers must still go out for the ones she loved: for Scott, and Megan and Michael.

We ask for the presence of this divine man Jesus, to be near us and watch with us as our Savior, someone who knew our grief and bore our sorrows, to bring his mercy and power to us, as we try to bow to Caitlyn being gone, as we pray that the unknown days before us bring no more wounds. And if we hold up our faith all mixed with outrage, and screaming within, that is just the heart's honesty and the mystery of God must sort them out.

We are in a passage of sorrow that can drive us to silence, where any speech can seem trivial. None of the consolations that we use to cushion death are available to us. But we are given words today, from prophets and saints, in prayers and hymns, that were set down at the edge of life, the edge that is blank to us and that we need the Spirit to cross: "the Lord is my shepherd"; "in his arms he'll take and shield you"; "grace will lead me home." We make ourselves speak of what we cannot see, and cannot grasp, because there is our hope.

Even memory, often so powerful and redemptive at death, as the old times come back, has been painful, shadowed by what will not be. It would be unbearable to list it all—yet we have, silently to ourselves, and in hushed voices to one another. This is the shadow of death, and we feel it. What we need to cling to, and it's hard to feel it, is God's promise: we have to say: "Yea, though I walk through the valley of the shadow of death . . . , you are with me, your rod and staff they comfort me."

When *I* remember Caitlyn, I always see her smiling. Just now, the memory of that smile can pierce the heart, but who will say it was not a gift? She was one of God's fresh creatures, whose face could light up in joy. She gave life to two children. What she brought to the earth is still among us, living in her children, living in our memories, though painful now, and we can't let them go.

She was, like us, a creature of earth, and we always walk in the shadow of death. We enliven it for each other. We have had to confront our terrible frailty—the frailty of our bodies, our families, our communities, how one moment can strike us all. We feel how cold the shadow can be, as we slip from one another. We have to feel the Lord walking with us, always, gathering us together, though we lose one another and ourselves, and preparing a place for us, to revive us and bring us to peace.

Here, in this place, we trade and give names in weddings and baptisms. They're part of a family's journey together. But we trade and give them as well before God, in the name of God, part of our journey through the earth, where we cannot rest forever, to the eternal home of God, where what was given here is restored, and treasured as here. There can't have been many young couples that started out from their wedding with more good will from everyone than Scott and Caitlyn did. We are now passing through a kind of earthquake, where what shouldn't have happened, did. We pray for that deeper naming to be firm and sure; we call on God to call Caitlyn by name and welcome her home.

Memory will not always be painful; it will be a lifeline. What we bring here in pain is an echo of the strong endurance of love. When we rush together in the face of tragedy, what we *see* is the tragedy, but what we *show* is care and love, the strength that binds us together. Part of us is gone with Caitlyn, but part of her remains with us. Your presence here is a testimony to love, and that is still real and still necessary. It's part of our strength on the earth, and we still need it.

Caitlyn loved this earth. She loved the seasons of nature, loved to hunt and fish. She loved earth's creatures, and a wandering animal could do no better than to fall into her hands, to be brought home, even on the sly, and cared for. She would recognize the image of hope drawn for us in Psalm 23: that there is some good shepherd who guides and provides. She would recognize that.

St. Paul says we don't live or die to ourselves—and that's true in many ways. What strikes one, strikes many. What one gives is for many. We are frail creatures, but we have also been given strength and courage and the power to love. We have to be strong and courageous in the face of what love has lost with Caitlyn. We have to be strong and courageous for Scott, and what love must still face. For Megan and Michael, those who are here out of Scott and Caitlyn's love. We still watch and wait, and we bear the burden of love together.

But Paul wants us to believe and know we don't bear it alone. For us, death and life are enemies, and we are helpless in their strife. But God is above them: we are God's people, whether we live or whether we die. This was Christ's victory, what his pain was for, to be the Lord of life and death and gather us out of our frailty into his strength.

We ask Jesus, who prayed to be spared, who wanted his loved ones near him, who bowed to what he had to do, we ask him to receive our prayers, to be near us with his power and help us bear what has come to us and will come. We ask him to show us that nothing can separate us from his love, and that we are together in him.

We commend Caitlyn to God's love and peace, to be welcomed lovingly and renewed. We cry out of our journey, shadowed by death, for the green pastures and still waters of God's peace. We cry for God's comfort: we need God's power to hold us up. May the Lord be with us, as we know the Lord is with Caitlyn, this young child of God. May we share one day the cup of joy at God's table. May God's mercy fill us now and may we one day dwell, as Caitlyn dwells, in the house of the Lord forever.

Amen.

IV. LOYAL

The readings for the service were:
Sirach 44: 1–15; Psalm 90; Revelation 21: 1–4; Luke 7: 1–10.
Bethel Lutheran, Karlstad, MN
December 28, 1995

I criticized, earlier, another pastor's funeral sermon for a mayor I had known well; I thought never mentioning his public life short-changed both his life and the community's life. This is the sermon I offered then as an example of how I would do it. As will be clear in the sermon, I picked the readings both for their ties to leadership, building, and responsibility and for their sense of labor across generations. Loyal belonged to a large family and he himself had a large family, many of them devoted to public service. He had an imposing presence and, if he were present at a meeting, you had best take notice of him. Not that you had to wait long for or guess at his opinion. One of my favorite memories of him was from an annual meeting. One of our more eccentric members had made a suggestion that was unusually ridiculous, even for him: he thought we should dissolve the church council, get rid of all the officers, and have the congregation as a whole decide everything together. There was a silence as people tried to think of some polite way to respond. Then, out of the silence, from the back row, boomed Loyal's deep voice: "Why, man, that's the stupidest idea I've ever heard."

We come before the Lord today with more loss and less urgent hope than these elders who came to Jesus, pleading a favor for another worthy man. For us, the cries for aid and the measure of what might be done are over now; they have given way to grief, memory, blessing, and solemn commendation. The man we lift to the Lord as worthy is gone from us, and we plead not for a servant but the man himself. And yet this man had something of the old Roman rectitude and public dedication we glimpse in the centurion whose faith amazed Jesus. And our elders and our people can praise him in almost identical terms: Lord, he is worthy of your attention; for he loved us and he helped build our community.

We bury a man today who was well-named: Loyal. He was a man of dogged loyalty and ferocious attachment. What was his was his forever: lived for and fought for as though it were the flesh that held his heart. His family, his friends, his church, his community—and I can hardly say "in that order," because it seemed to all go together for Loyal; we were all part of him, and he gave us all his unquestioning, if sometimes contentious, devotion.

He loved the people he worked with, and it wasn't hard to love him back. This last year, as he went from one institution to another, I don't think I've ever heard so many doctors, nurses, and aides praised so highly. They were all wonderful. Though he had to take the orders now and not give them—well, I hear he still gave a few—and though he grumbled about falling into the hands of the Gestapo, he loved the people that cared for him. If you found your way into his heart, that soft old heart, you stayed there.

When we first came here, he was sitting on the Bethel Church Council and he looked the perfect image of a governing elder, someone who could have talked strategy with Moses and who would abide no nonsense. When I first heard him bark out one of his concise observations, I thought: if he had a cigar, he could be Winston Churchill, risen up to do battle again. He had the same strong-jawed and hawk-eyed dignity, the same imperial presence. But if you put a grandchild in his arms or said a prayer with him, you would see him cry like a baby.

I probably knew him when he had mellowed a little. He joked to me once that he had given up arguing seriously about politics after he started having heart attacks. Of course, once or twice, I had to think: boy, I wonder what he sounded like when he was arguing *seriously*. But he seemed to me a large souled man, alive to the complexities of life, how it isn't always as neat as we would like it to be, how its sloppy loyalties sometimes mock us.

I heard an echo of Loyal in this centurion who comes to Jesus for help. The centurion is famous for his humility: others claim he is worthy; but, before Jesus, he says, "Lord, I am not worthy you should come under my roof." Yet, side by side with that humility before Jesus, that yielding to the majesty *of God*, that sense of his own unworthiness to ask a *divine* favor, there is also a strong, commanding nature, somebody that's used to working in the public world—and used to getting his way. The centurion has absolute faith in the word of Jesus because, he says, he knows a little something about giving orders himself: "I say to one 'Go' and he goes; and to another 'Come' and he comes; and to my slave 'Do this' and the slave does it." I can almost hear Loyal saying that, especially if he were explaining to you how simple something was. But I can hear him say, too, "Lord, I am not worthy that you should come under my roof."

And yet that public life, that willingness to lead and command, was very much a part of Loyal and something we do see as one of the fruits of our faith, one way faith works in the world. It's something that today we both lament in his passing and celebrate in his life—public service, civic responsibility.

The great English architect, Christopher Wren, is buried in St. Paul's Cathedral in London, one of the churches he designed. And near his tomb is a tablet that says: "If you seek his monument, look about you." Gathered here in the middle of Karlstad, the town Loyal loved and served as mayor for so long, we might, if more modestly, say the same. He was intensely proud of its public works and physical beauty, that highway he worked to straighten, the hospital, the nursing home, the wide streets, and the handsome approaches. Here was the embodiment of that old civic virtue, the dignity and integrity that found its own flesh in the sticks and stones of buildings, the investment in common life, community institutions and services.

When the book of Sirach praises famous men, it is praising that investment in time, the life of the past that became a gift for the future, the instruction and counsel and effort that became a people's heritage. It's a hymn to the continuity of earthly life, the traditions that free us from the prison of the present and make us mindful of consequences and responsibilities, and it's an acknowledgement that in each generation people must step forward to make that investment.

It was something Loyal honored in others. If you knew him, you knew of his family's achievements in school, church, the military, the law, public service. He used to joke that there were so many lawyers and pilots in his family, if the lawyers couldn't keep him out of trouble, the pilots could fly him to Cuba—as though anyone could imagine this staunch old Republican living in Cuba! But he valued public service.

Of course, communities change. We are not masters of time but servants in it. You could see in Loyal sometimes the fighting spark of the old warrior when he contemplated some of the changes. Many of us, no doubt, have heard him growl, "Where there's a will, there's a way," and we might silently have thought: well, maybe not always.

Every monument will crumble in time, even as our bodies do, or become unattended or incomprehensible to the strange children of the future. We are all children of earth and will return to the dust.

Our loyalties must finally rest in a smaller scope and we find ourselves clinging to each other like leaves of grass that are easily consumed. I said Loyal took pride in the achievements of his family, and he did: but nothing could have stopped him from loving them. If you did put a grandchild in his arms, you might have thought he was nobody but Grandpa Oistad who had never worried about anything but making a baby smile.

We come to a limit and then we must bow, as the centurion did, as we do today, to the Lord of time. We must take refuge, with all the generations, in the graciousness of the Lord.

Loyal was blessed, and we were blessed in him, with a long life, rounded off with deep satisfaction. He had become so frail, and he didn't want to leave his home again. When he was in the nursing home, lying with his legs crossed on his bed, watching his beloved baseball, he would say with finality—after praising the nursing home and its staff, "But *I* don't belong here," and you would almost believe him; he wanted you to believe him. He couldn't believe anyone could object to him driving—he who had driven more miles than anyone in the county! He wanted you to believe he was the same man who had driven all those miles. It was as though he were telling his own body: where there's a will, there's a way.

The will and the spirit might have been there. But the flesh had come to its end. He had come home. He went on his last hunt. He saw his children, and theirs, and theirs. He rejoined his treasured community and was allowed to let it know his mind for a little while again. The time had simply come for him to go in peace. And, in peace, he left us.

We send him now to that heavenly city, the new Jerusalem, shining with the radiance of a rare jewel, bright as crystal. He would have found it fitting to imagine paradise as a city, where the people are gathered and their deepest satisfactions found. But, in this city, God will wipe away every tear, and sorrow and death will be no more.

It's a city that claimed Loyal's faith and claims our faith even here, God dwelling with us. We gather as family, friends, elders, and citizens today, but we gather here as members of God's temple, people of faith.

We sing today songs of Christmas yearning, Christmas joy, and Christmas peace. We have pondered, again this season, the descent of God to us, the sending of angels, the sending of God's son.

What we offer on our part, in service throughout life, and what we send to God today, in the person of one dear to us, is human life in all its beauty and perplexity. We claim the Lord's loving welcome for Loyal, a lovable, exasperating, dedicated, stubborn, dignified, sweet, playful, and faithful man. He was a gift to us, and we give him now to the Lord who gave, and who will give *him* eternal life.

And we do sing of joy. Joy for a life well-lived and well-loved. Joy for our lives with their sorrows and their blessings. Joy for our world, to which Christ came, who took on our flesh in his time, to redeem us for all time. We commend Loyal to his hands, and to the great wonder of his undying love.

Amen.

V. RAYMOND

The readings for the service were:
Ecclesiastes 3: 1–15; Psalm 85; Romans 8: 31–39; Luke 23: 32–33, 39–43.
Zion Lutheran, Lake Bronson, MN
October 7, 1989

When I was speaking of feeling bound to acknowledge, sometimes, the harsher or bleaker sides of a person's life and character, this is the sermon I spoke of as having tied me up in knots. I knew three generations of the family quite well; they were active in the church and the community and were easy-going, likable people. The dead man I knew not at all; I think it even came as a surprise to me that this first husband, father, and grandfather of the people I knew had been still alive. And I believe it was only at the time of his death that I learned how rough things had been before they split up. I don't recall learning much more than that but I have the strong sense things really were bad. I can't imagine what led me to choose, for the gospel, the story of the two criminals being crucified with Jesus, but I like the mixture of anger and grace at the point of death. If I hadn't known the family so well, I might have hesitated to use something so unusual and gone for something more bland. Ecclesiastes was here not for its scope but for its list of dark and painful times as part of life. Psalm 85 and Romans 8 both strongly proclaim forgiveness and mercy. Reading this sermon now, it strikes me as unusually abstract and reflective but I know I was assuming those who knew Raymond would hear it with the mixed and troubled emotions I was trying to speak to. But it did tie me in knots so that my strongest memory is the relief I felt when his daughter thanked me.

We gather today around the same fate that has claimed all the children of earth: the saints, the sinners, and even the Savior. What was meant as a gesture of mockery in the crucifixion is really the enactment of a profound truth: for Jesus Christ, for the nameless criminals, for all those in between, death is there to be met somehow. We see in this one moment of the crucifixion story a little community to which death has come. We see how it loosens the tongues of both anger and kindness. We hear a cry of anger and desperation. We hear a rough estimate of justice. We hear a plea to be remembered. And we hear a word of mercy and promise.

Voices and cries and words like these fill our lives, as we grope for what we want and need from one another. But, at life's end, they claim our attention with an urgency that is difficult to satisfy. Death seems to set us a confusing question and we fumble for an answer in utter confusion. It issues us a common challenge: to meet it somehow, to find something to say to one another, to heed memory and to search for mercy.

Death has the power to call to us across space and time. And each death reaches out to touch those who were part of the life it ended, with the most personal of invitations. Raymond's death, occurring half a continent away, has called out more clearly than any number of deaths somewhat nearer could have. It has that power because his life was part of the life that goes on here, of what has been shared, of what has been remembered.

I don't know that anyone could ever say what they really feel at times like this. Feelings wage war in us, rise and fall, cancel each other out. With so final a thing as death, something so beyond our ordinary affairs, we can be as speechless as we are before the sun's rising or a furious blizzard. And the touch of a life upon us is itself so confused and so confusing we may never be able to give it adequate expression.

It's the rare life that can be summed up definitely, one way or another. Like the three men on the crosses on Calvary, we are a mixture of this and that, good and bad: what is true of us at one minute may not be true of us at the next. And we give ourselves to each other with all our mixed-up complications, knowing as little what we're giving as what we're getting.

Families make us the most intimate of friends and the most intimate of enemies, usually some of both. We may never be able to say which we are more. We become too much a part of one another for judgments to make much sense. But what is undeniable is that we become attached, with all the mysterious force that life can bring. So attached that we can never mistake which cries to be remembered are addressed to us.

That famous passage we read from Ecclesiastes says that there is a time for everything—and it means everything, with the most unblinking honesty: keeping and casting away; killing and healing; loving and hating; war and peace. In our lives together, we find the time for most of them, in one form or another. As long as life lasts, there is the hope or the fear that there may yet be time for something else.

But there is also a time to die, the limit of our time together, a time when we must gather as we have today and, like the men on Calvary, say something final out of all the things that lie deep within us.

Coming here is part of our answer to the call of death, to the call of this death. We can say that Ray's death issued a final claim and that we have accepted it; we can say that his death issued a cry to be remembered and that we have heard it.

But being here we put forth our own claim and our own cry: we claim the attention of God for Ray and we cry out for God to remember him and receive him into eternal life.

We ask for the gift of boundless compassion. We ask for something none of us could earn but that all of us need. And we ask in confidence because we ask in the name of Christ.

When Jesus told the man who hung beside him, "Today you will be with me in paradise," we can see how boundless his compassion was. The gift was given almost for the asking. One kind word, which we might even call more accurate than kind, was enough. But this is the measure of God. We could scarcely begin to measure our own lives, but the one who can seems to measure them with the greatest forgiveness and the greatest love. Of all the moments of this man's life, which he doesn't bother to tally or to excuse, one kind word, at the bitter end, was enough.

We want a lot more from each other. What we get, much of the time, is only a kind of cease-fire. But the words of Jesus want to put us on the path of real peace, lead us to where mercy and truth meet, where righteousness and peace kiss, where the confused truth of the earth shall be covered with the righteousness of heaven.

Coming before this loving God, gathering here to claim the voice of Christ as our own, is more than a response to death. It is our claim of victory over all the voices death lets loose, our grasp of mercy and the promise of salvation. We offer at Ray's end the last gesture of love and kindness: we commend him to the arms of God. We place him and we place ourselves under the cross where mercy and truth meet, where the confusions of life and death are touched by the grace of salvation.

Amen.

VI. JAMES

The readings for the service were:
Isaiah 40: 27–31; Psalm 130; Romans 8: 31–39; Mark 14: 32–36a.
Faith Lutheran, Eagle Bend, MN
February 21, 2009

This was another painful funeral for a man I knew little of. He had been living out West, looking for a better life than our little town offered. But he lost what he had when our economy sank, grew desperate, and took his own life. The family requested "On Eagles' Wings" as one of the hymns, which led me to choose the Isaiah passage. The outcry of Psalm 130, with its desperation, its brooding over sin, and its waiting in the night seemed to me words we needed to speak and hear. I again used Jesus's sorrow in Gethsemane as a bond to our recoiling from what was before us; but I stopped short and ended midway through verse thirty-six, at his prayer to be spared, which I repeated as I began the sermon.

He fell on the ground and prayed that . . . the hour might pass from him. And he said, "Father, remove this cup from me . . ."

 This desperate prayer has risen from countless souls in agony, in like words or in silent yearning, when life wavers at the approach of what seems unbearable, courage slips away, and mercy is asked from time and circumstance, pardon is begged from the future. We have prayed it for ourselves and we have prayed it for those we love, that the hour of terror might pass like the mist of night, and a clear dawn might find us safe somehow, unharmed somehow, on the other side of desperation, the other side of pain.

 And this moment, when the soul of Jesus sorrowed, even to death, has found a special place in the Christian heart, so that it has been rendered on church wall and window and hung over Christian altars. Its image is over the entrance to our nave.

The place called Gethsemane will forever stand for the moment when the *Lord* of life trembled at what life was bringing, the Lord of time wished time away, the obedient one raised one cry of regret. This is a place where the humanity of Jesus embraces our own, the moment we cry out at where life has brought us, cry out against what is claiming us.

We here are in the grip of two bitter hours, that we might wish had never to be: this long hour of grief, from the news of last week to whenever time can soothe memory, when we mourn the death of someone beloved, who shared the work and shared the joy of this community, who went out with high hopes to a new life. And that other, first short hour, when James turned from life to death. We would have both pass from us, by somehow forestalling the first. But though we go back to that moment, with our blind guessing, in pain or wonder or fear or confusion, it stays beyond our power, as James is, and we are left with its burden.

Timely deaths have their own consolations—long years savored, lingering illness avoided. Sudden, early deaths have few: and death that is chosen is loss at its most unacceptable, it brings mourning at its most inconsolable.

It's as though the very life we share has been assaulted, assaulted so seriously and so completely that we ourselves are left defenseless.

We want someone or something to blame, because we're looking for sense, we're rewriting the moments of our past, we're fighting an accusation we feel; we want some agent we can punish or judge for things done or left undone. But all the verdicts can sound so empty. They're coming more from our anger and our hurt than our wisdom. It's death, finally, that is our real enemy, how unforgiving it is and final: death and its shadow, despair, that can so darken our way we're lost within it.

The mysteries here go deeper than verdicts and judgments, deeper than words. The human spirit is such a maze; we find ourselves peering into its most hidden places, as helpless as if we tried to gaze to the bottom of the ocean. It's no wonder our spirits are in turmoil and distress. We don't know how James came to be where he was; we guess but we don't know what he felt, what he thought, what he meant, what he hoped. We hardly know what we feel.

But even if we were granted complete understanding, I don't know if it would help much. Understanding isn't all we want. We'd still be left with the coldness of loss, an hour that came and will never go away. It's just the fact of it that's overwhelming: nothing else can tell us anything to equal that. We already know the worst.

In a way, our confusion or anger or fear or agitation, our not knowing, the darkness of our understanding, will bring us as *close to* understanding as we can get.

We read Psalm 130 for its cry from the depths, and much of its power comes from its remaining a sheer outcry, without request and without answer. It's a human voice seeking the ear of God, reaching first for a communion that soothes the soul.

But the most profound part of that psalm is when it says: "If you were to keep watch over sins—O Lord, who could stand?" Our hurts lead us to our failings: our healing is bound up with forgiveness: and forgiveness is needed by all. And it's a word of communion with us, and a guidance for us, that the voice in the psalm is of a soul still waiting for morning, waiting in the night, but waiting in hope.

Part of the sadness of our nature is that our very strengths can so often turn against us. As James was remembered this week, everyone spoke of his charm, his energy, working and taking charge, always busy, his ebullience, not wanting to share worries, his eagerness to act and settle things, and all of it full speed ahead. All good things for so much of life. But those very qualities, when your way is blocked, can isolate you, frustrate you, burden and torment you. They can bring you to a moment and a desperate choice that's unforgiving and final.

And now this choice and this moment are ours, too. What then shall we say? We have the longer hour to bear—we can't make it pass from us any more than Jesus could. What shall we say?

When St. Paul spoke his all-encompassing list of all that could *not* separate us from God, he mentioned both death *and* life. Death, so final a separation from everything, could not sever us from the love of God. Those are words of profound hope. But that other word shows an even more profound hope and proclaims an even greater mercy: that our *life* cannot separate us from the love of God. Our life, whatever its confusions and mistakes, our life, whatever burdens it acquires, our life can never be a barrier to God's love.

A death like this can present us with that feeling of harsh separation, rejection. Your coming here proclaims there is no separation from your love either. The witness of this gathering is to testify to a deeper reality, a bond of acceptance, a communion that refuses all barriers to love. We gather to commend James, in loving memory, to the grace and mercy of God. We gather, too, because we need God's grace. In death, and in life.

We need it to take us to the other side of desperation. At Gethsemane, when Jesus lifted up his desperate prayer, he also said: "Father, all things are possible to you." He meant: God should spare him his pain. God didn't. And yet he was right: all things were possible with God. God didn't spare him his pain, but God brought him through his pain, through death, through desperation, to new life.

We all need that gracious guidance—through death and through life. It's the mystery that lies on the other side of the mysteries that perplex us, that takes us through them, the mystery of grace. We here say grace is mercy, blessing, God's free gift of love; but it also names one of our qualities—grace: beauty of movement.

And we can say that James stumbled on his way and that his stumbling brought us here awkwardly and clumsily. What we need, what we are promised, is the sure touch of this divine hand, the God of mercy who will steady us, and never let go of us, however we wander, however we fall, whatever the weight we bear, who will lift us up to light and freedom.

Amen.

VII. WAYNE

The readings for the service were:
Ecclesiastes 3: 1–14; Psalm 23; Philippians 4: 4–9; John 14: 1–6, 27.
Faith Lutheran, Eagle Bend, MN
November 15, 2008

I wanted to close this section with another person who died a fairly peaceful death after a long and productive life. If we all lived and died as Wayne did, we would have an easy time agreeing that dying is only a part of living, and we'd never scream about the injustice and savagery of it. The serene and soothing passages that are listed in all the handbooks seem to have been written for the occasion. I've often called the Philippians passage the charter of Christian humanism and pointed out that the qualities Paul recommends we think about don't necessarily have our label on them. This was especially appropriate for Wayne because, though he was a member and many in his family were active in the church, he really was not. He's one of the people I knew well from community, not church, activities. I also knew his spouse well; she was a teacher and a great reader and we often met and chatted at the library. But she had remained a member of a different church and, for Wayne's funeral, requested that her own pastor also preach. He gave one of the strangest funeral sermons I've ever heard, and I was again left brooding about how little I understood human beings.

We have felt, lately, the turning of the seasons of the earth: grey skies, chilly winds rustling bare branches, icy rain and snow, have come upon us. The birds and the deer, men and women, have joined in their autumn rituals, shiftings and chases as old as time. The year is falling to its end, and nature is folding into itself.

It's a time when our thoughts, our lives, our steps, turn to warmth and home, gathering for the holidays, but really gathering against the cold and the dark, to light the way for each other by being together.

We gather today with the same unspoken drawing near and clinging close of the children of earth. The coldness and darkness of death have come among us and taken one of our own. We come in solemn attendance for Wayne's passing, out of loss but more deeply: out of love. We gather, as well, as people of faith, before God and within *God's* love, to give thanks for Wayne, to bless his memory, and commend him to the love that created and sustained him.

In its most famous words, Ecclesiastes tells us there's time for everything, but first, and as our limits, a time to be born and a time to die. The last time is promised to us when we're given the first. But death came to Wayne so swiftly, we felt its alien and intrusive nature with great force. There's probably no one here who didn't say last week: "But I just saw him! I thought he was doing well." And yet, there's a strange mercy there: we *did* just see him, leaning on the counter at Farm and Lumber, driving his truck, visiting and storytelling, and we always will see him that way: never lingering as he loses his powers, loses the fullness of his life. It's as though he just walked out of the room into a greater life because he knew it was time to go.

He was certainly a great presence in our community's life. One of the strongest memories I have of Wayne is a public one: I see him loping along in the Memorial Day parade with the flag, walking with that easy rambling gait that looked like it was made for the long haul. I probably remember that because he was telling me once, before the parade, how many of them he'd marched in and how much it meant to him.

He was a pillar of the town's life and business; I see him most typically somewhere around Farm and Lumber, the business that was so much a part of him. I see him with that little settling of himself he'd do before he told a story or shared a philosophical reflection, keeping his smile in reserve, but helplessly letting his eye twinkle out his good humor.

He had one of those lives that gave our small towns their character, most of his years lived out not that far from right here, one part of a long family endeavor. And Wayne was one of those priceless community builders, who don't have to bend everything to their will, who do their work as one worker among many. He could receive and cherish what was handed down to him and hand on his trust in turn, then step aside.

That quiet work and sensitivity, that appreciation of the efforts of others, was part of his sheer love of other people. He loved the pageantry of life, watching lives flourish. You can't tell Wayne's story without filling it with other people: his family, his friends, all he was part of. And you can't really tell it without saying just how pleasant it always was to have him around.

When Paul calls us, in Philippians, to rejoice always, he knows as much as any of us that he calls us to joy in the face of the world's losses and its sorrows. He's trying to lead us to peace within this life, and he thinks we can get there by gentleness, thanksgiving, patience, and by a life that's confident and generous enough to be open to the lives around it: whatever is just, pleasing, whatever is commendable and worthy of praise.

Wayne had a lot of those qualities: he had an ear for *your* life: he respected the lives of others, the rights they had to their ways. He was settled with life itself: he had that peace about him.

And he departed in peace. He told me once, not that long ago, that he was struck sometimes by how many things people feared that they didn't have to. When he learned human skill could do no more for him, it was as though his spirit took that knowledge and, without fear or regret, moved on.

We're in the wake of that swift departure: but if we can take a step back (and we will, with the healing of time) and consider his long, rich life, active, vibrant, loving and being loved, using his gifts, being himself a great gift, we can declare: he really did have a good one.

We commend him now to the very kingdom of joy and peace. We claim for him those beautiful, simple promises of Jesus: "I'll prepare a place for you—I'll come and take you to myself." Someone as down to earth and sociable as Wayne could ask for no better welcome.

And we ask God to surround us with that same love, to soothe our loss of this life we give thanks for. And may the peace of God, which passes all understanding, keep our hearts and minds in Christ Jesus.

Amen.

VIII

One of the strange gifts of loss, even tragic loss, is that you see emerging around you, from the people you've been living next to for years, a small community of fellow sufferers, those who've lived through what you're living through. A kind of instant, ad hoc support group, that you never imagined existed, steps forward to touch you and share your burdens. Anyone who's ever managed to find a group like that knows how irreplaceable it is, or how unusual it can be, to be with people who don't diminish what you're saying because they know what you're talking about. I certainly wouldn't say that congregations can replace intentional support groups, but the small congregations I served offered similar gifts.

After funerals, congregations re-form and go back to their ordinary lives. I said earlier that the funeral rite and the funeral assembly gained strength from being so similar to the Sunday assembly and its regular worship. The same is true for the worship that follows the funeral: it's a source of strength, definition, and stability, all the more powerful for not having to be invented for the occasion. The visits I made to the grieving, in some cases, only continued the visits I'd been making to the aging, home-bound couple whom death had come to.

Congregations reform, but their pasts slowly drift away. As I read over the sermons I proclaimed at funerals, details I touched on or alluded to that must have been alive, often painfully, to me and everyone hearing me, are now beyond my grasp. I can see Caitlyn and Scott as clearly as though I were still bumping into them every week, but I've lost all memory of their children and what they went through at the time.

Even with all our means of preservation, we fall away from each other into the past.

In every congregation we served, there was a prominent display of confirmation class pictures. You could trace many of the local families back through several generations. Especially at funerals, when long departed relatives returned, these pictures always had people clustered around them, searching out faces themselves or pointing them out to their children. At the first church we served, however, the collection had been destroyed when the church burned down, ten years before we arrived. Someone suggested, as the church's ninetieth anniversary was approaching, that we reconstitute the collection to mark the event. We sent letters to everyone connected with the church whom we had an address for, asking if they had confirmation pictures we could copy somehow. The response was amazing; we managed to collect pictures of most, if not all, of our confirmation classes.

The problem we then had was in naming the students pictured. The further we went back toward the church's beginning the more faces there were that our current members couldn't recognize. The first few years were left with several gaps. Even though we had the church books, they didn't help us tell which of fifteen girls and twelve boys in any given picture was which. I think it was our financial secretary that solved this: she reminded us that one of our oldest and most widely connected members, Hjalmar Johnson, was still pretty sharp, even though bound to a nursing home and over ninety. If anybody could give us the names, he could.

We went there late one afternoon. I'll never forget sitting there in the fading light, in that overly warm room, Hjalmar slumped in his easy chair, our secretary holding up pictures in front of him, as his long shaking finger tapped child after child and he recited the names without hesitation. It was like the past rising and reaching out to us for one last farewell. Hjalmar died a few months later. If he hadn't given the names, they would have vanished.

And yet they're vanishing anyway. The names may be neatly typed below the faces but the sense of who these young people were is quickly fading as they, their contemporaries, their children, their grandchildren, and all the rest of us age and die.

One of the hymns we use on the Feast of All Saints is Ralph Vaughan Williams's magnificent setting of the text "For All the Saints." But the tune itself is called *Sine Nomine*, "Without Name," which always seemed fitting to me. We know well some of the names and even some of the quirks of the early Christians like Peter, James, John, Luke, Paul, Barnabas, and Stephen, as we know those near to us, our pastors and teachers, our parents and our classmates, the people that sit around us in the pews. But between that heroic past and our ordinary present there is a long, living rope of Christians, nameless and faceless for us, who helped make our lives what they are.

And Christians, of course, only share the human lot. Something like this is true for all of us, for every community, every family.

Mary Carol and I are in a few of those confirmation pictures. In one of them, I have a furious expression, my eyes are narrowing, my body is leaning forward, and my mouth is opening, as though I am about to scream at the photographer and leap for his throat. People that knew me are probably chuckling at this, and visitors might pause to wonder what on earth I was doing. But, not that many years from now, there will be fewer to stop and laugh, then fewer, than hardly any at all, who will bother to wonder or even to look.

PART FOUR

Without Form and Void

I

Silence and solitude, conditions hard to find and hard to rest in during my church service, fill the days of my retirement. I'm enjoying them.

I would often say I was tired of talking and sick of hearing my own voice. I gained sympathy for politicians who spend a lifetime talking in public, inevitably saying things that are embarrassingly false, thoughtless, overgeneralized, hasty, too extreme, too mild, simply stupid, or taken by someone (or many someones) as unforgivable insults, then needing another lifetime to heal the words with more words, inevitably inadequate. It's nice, finally, not to worry about speaking for the record. It's nice, at last, to shut up. I speak so little now I sometimes trip over my words when I do try to talk. After over fifty years of marriage, Mary Carol and I can read each other's minds. So there are days when the creature I speak to the most is our dog Yum-Yum.

She's named for the bride in Gilbert and Sullivan's *The Mikado*. (Our last dog was named Patience, and the one before Sullivan.) Yum-Yum is the fifth dog we've lived with, one of those short lives that pierce your heart when they're hurt, when they suffer, when they die. If you need reminding of the shortness of life and the misery of losing what you love, join your life to a dog's. They offer a more powerful *memento mori* than a skull at a banquet and you won't be tempted to joke when they lay dying. Yum-Yum is probably nearing her end. She looks placidly out at the world she once barked furiously at and ran about wildly in. She's had two serious dizzy spells this year (oddly like spells I had, which I'll discuss later): she staggered about, fell over, managed to rise and get to one of her safe spots (under the piano bench), then lay there shaking in terror.

But she still loves her walks, her runs which are no longer really runs, and lying in the yard, surveying the neighborhood and greeting the folks (and the dogs) that pass. She doesn't, however, much like being out there alone, so she's ended up shaping my days as much as silence and solitude have. We got her from a rescue shelter shortly after retiring, and I very soon gave in to her need to be together outside, sitting near her on a bench Mary Carol bought for me, under a gingko tree. I do a great part of my reading and writing there (or, well, here). In the summer, Yum-Yum and I turn through the hours with the gingko's shade, like living parts of a sundial. Winter, unfortunately, only attracts Yum-Yum more, and we're out there until the temperature drops below freezing, me shivering in my parka, Yum-Yum in bliss.

We walked out one frigid, raw, and chilly day, a day of dark clouds and gusting winds, to our tree and bench, and I saw one of our neighbors outside, reporting some vandalism to a police officer. Meeting him later, I said I hoped the officer hadn't thought I was being nosy. My neighbor laughed and said he'd told him we were always out there. He added: "He just thought you were crazy."

I live a fairly simple, fairly static, almost monastic life. Just after we retired, when we would still occasionally attend the meetings of the conference pastors, we were all discussing changes in congregations and somehow began discussing "reinventing" ourselves. We did that pointless, time-burning exercise of going around the table, each of us noting some act of self-reinvention. I said I was reinventing myself as a hermit. As always, when I state the blunt truth, everyone thought I was kidding.

But becoming a hermit wouldn't be a bad description of how my life has changed. Thomas Merton, the talkative Trappist hermit, had been an inspiration for me when I was young. I enjoyed his writing and had used one of his books (*Faith and Violence*) when I taught a course in ethics. But I also admired the life behind the writings: the life of a contemplative, a life spent in quietness, devoted to reading and writing. Much of the life I lived as a parish pastor cut very much against the grain of my natural inclinations: the constant but necessary engagement with people, the public exposure. When I did my internship, I told my supervisor that I ended a lot of days feeling bruised. It was a feeling I would get to know well.

So it's nice to dwell in solitude, and to feel, no doubt as many aging people do, that I'm becoming more myself. Some days I miss the rigid, structured routines of parish life, each day bringing its own tasks, all bending with the cycle of Sundays and church seasons. But I wouldn't go back: just looking at church office calendars makes my stomach flip. And the things I treasured in church life (or life itself), the art, the music, the scholarship, are still part of my life and work. I mark my days with Matins, Vespers, and Compline, probably more faithfully than I did when I was fighting for time in my office. I do some volunteering but, again, I like to do things where my contact with people is minimal, like playing the piano when my church holds care center services or washing sheets for our homeless shelter.

I supply preach fairly regularly, but, here as well, I start to draw back from anything more extended or more serious. Supplying too often, you start to sense people are on the point of asking you to visit the hospital, or even preside at funerals. Of course, they should: presiding at worship should lead to shepherding and all that means. But then it's time for me to go. I don't want to wade into the raw grief of others again; I don't want to walk into another hospital room. I don't want to engage with anyone at that level. A pastor we know, who serves a church large enough to have four services each weekend and really could use an assistant, sent me a note wondering if I'd consider doing some home visitation or hospital calls. He told me when he got my reply he laughed out loud, because he'd never received so violently definite a refusal.

But this marks one of the greatest changes in my life now: far less of my time is claimed by death and all it brings. I had, for this writing project, re-read all my funeral sermons, and the reading brought back what a constant that was in my life, and what an emotional burden. I realized how happy I was, in early retirement, moving hundreds of miles away from where I served, to know no one well enough to feel bound to attend a funeral. I was hoping to be done with death, at least for a time. (This has, of course, begun to change. When hymns are used, at the funerals we now attend, that we used a lot in our services, I can barely sing them.)

I sometimes wonder what any of it amounted to, all my thinking, all my words. But that strikes me as one of those self-dramatizing questions that there's no sensible way to answer. It's like asking what your life as a whole was worth: the judgment's not ours to make. I hope, in my ministry to mourners, I was able to bring some light, some grace, something of value, that I was at least part of the community's effort to make its way to whatever was next.

But all the hospital vigils, living with and knowing well so many people as they lived their last years, the forced and formal meditations on death, certainly had an effect on me. It was a great part of what made me the person I am as I wait for and wonder about my own death. It made death an indelible dark line across any future I pictured. It impressed me beyond all denial and all forgetting with the vulnerability and frailty of the flesh, all the ways our lives, our loves, and our bodies can come apart. I learned the power of time, its relentless passing, the well of darkness it drags after us.

I think, too, that all of my service as a pastor shaped me toward the simple, static, and almost monastic life I live. Beneath all the sayings and doings of Jesus, there's a force in him for a simple life, a scorn for wealth, power, and glory, a calming of desire, a deflation of the proud self. Prolonged exposure to Jesus soaks you pretty thoroughly in that atmosphere. You see, clear as noon on a cloudless day, the futility of the things that are on earth.

Now that my official tasks are done, I no longer face death actively, as someone with a mission, called to act for others in its presence; I face death only as one more creature it will surely come to, and nothing I say or do will stay its coming.

My father died about ten years after my mother's death. He had had a paralyzing stroke and, in the early morning before I was to leave for Chicago, my sister called with the news he had died. I would not be driving home for a visit, but for his funeral.

I had jumped out of bed and run to answer the phone without bothering with the lights. I was standing there in the dark, and I felt a strong, cold wind blow into my face and across the top of my head. It was as though I had become the tallest person on earth, my head sticking up exposed above the clouds, waiting for the next strike that would come along. It was a shock of mortality, a helpless realization that, with both parents dead, my place in creation had changed.

As the years left to me grow shorter, that place is shown to me increasingly by the vulnerability and frailty of my own flesh, the failures of my own body. I could no longer be the healthy professional who travelled effortlessly at night to sit with his dying parishioners. I've led a privileged and a lucky life, a reasonably long and fairly healthy life, but time bears us all away, and the shadow death casts around me now is looking more and more like my own.

II

I actually had to make the naked choice once: whether I wanted to live or to die. I thought it was a revelatory moment, even though it happened in an encounter with a ghost.

I've encountered two. The second one was pretty primitive, and it was more of a dark presence rather than anything that might be called a ghost. This happened in the last parish we served, a place more than capable of spawning evil spirits. I woke in the middle of the night and thought the room around me looked strange. Then I noticed, across the room, against the outside wall, a great, dark, squarish lump, about twice the size of a clothes hamper. It was deep black, blacker than anything else in the room, and it seemed to be slowly pulsing and radiating a frosty chill. It certainly chilled me, and I lay there motionless, wondering how I could drive it off. I had no doubt this thing was evil and, like any good student of the New Testament, I knew the name of Jesus had power over all things evil. On the other hand, I remembered Jesus driving the devils into the Gadarene swine—as well as all the fairy-tales that warn of the disastrously literal obedience of spirits—so I worried about how exactly to word my exorcism. I didn't want to send it somewhere it might really hurt somebody. That I could lie there debating with myself the proper formulation for casting out demons makes me wonder how seriously I took this thing. In any case, I decided the *status quo ante* was probably the best solution, so I said (or did I just think?): "In the name of Jesus Christ, I command you to return to where you've come from." The dark shape seemed to grow taller and, with an audible breath or burst of wind, vanished right through the wall, and the room returned to its normal temperature.

The first ghost I encountered, much earlier in our service, was harder and more harrowing to deal with because it was the ghost of my mother. This happened very shortly after she died. I was, again, lying in bed. I didn't think I'd fallen quite asleep yet, though Mary Carol, as usual, had. I glanced down at the foot of the bed, and there was my mother, looking down on us. She was wearing, oddly, a bright green coat, which I'd never seen her in, with her arms crossed, holding it closed. The green color was dazzling, even though the lights were off and the room was dark. But I could see her clearly. She was staring intently at me. I rose on my elbows, and I said, "Mom? What are you doing here?"

My question seemed to energize her, or maybe she had just been waiting for me to notice her. She turned and walked up my side of the bed. I remember being puzzled as she approached me. I said, "But . . . you're dead." She opened wide her coat and leaned over me, covering my face and smothering me. The truth came to me like a lightning flash: she was going to kill me and take me down to her grave. I was choking and staring into absolute darkness. I threw my arms out and screamed, "No!" I felt like I was physically fighting my way from beneath the earth, back to the surface where the living were. Then she was gone, and I was sitting up, breathing heavily but breathing.

(To add one more oddity to this story, my mother isn't buried in the earth. She was terrified at the idea of lying underground, so she's in an above-ground vault.)

Whatever this experience might say about buried emotions and unresolved struggles, what stands out for me now is my instinctive fight for life. It wasn't something I weighed or thought about: it was an affirmation of living roaring up from the depths of my being. I wanted to live. And here I am, thirty years and more later, still at it.

I wonder if I would answer the same way, with the same force, today. Maybe it would depend on who had come back to drag me out of life. I've known spouses who died fairly soon after their partners, as though they had been summoned to follow and never thought twice about going.

It isn't only life we want: it's life with all the things and all the people we love. We live toward the future with the illusion that we'll all be going on together indefinitely. It's an illusion that can hardly survive childhood, but an illusion so powerful, shaped so perfectly to our deepest yearnings, that it mocks our knowledge and makes every tragic loss come upon us as an overwhelming shock.

Some of the peace that can come with age comes, I think, from this illusion finally weakening and losing its power to blind us so completely. It's certainly not something you have to fight very hard to overcome. You feel how thin the hope of tomorrow becomes daily. You easily see through the certainty of your cherished and thoughtless expectations. What's certain now is the end of all of them. But the time left toward that end always threatens to unravel, to devolve into chaos, to become without form and void.

There should be an orderly ritual for old age, something like the standard Christian communion service, which concentrates and sets in order the life a Christian lives. We need something that would take us through the days and years in some sort of sensible progression—meaning, I suppose, no surprises and only losses we're well-prepared for—and then leave us at the funeral home. As it is, the rituals of aging are: doctor visits, trips to the emergency room, hospital stays, rehab schedules, chronic pain management, and the funerals of others, all coming at random. (And that's if you're healthy and lucky.)

I keep my church rituals, and our family life has its own set of simple routines: meals, dog walks, gardening, hours for reading, working away at our own projects. But all these are vulnerable and easily overpowered by the real rituals of aging I listed above. We've had our trips to the emergency room: severed tendon, broken wrist from a fall, sliced knuckle, the simple attacks of the ordinary. And, even when we're not injuring ourselves, I carry around far too much knowledge of the body's misadventures to ever be quite at ease. I can't step into the shower without thinking of the people I've known who've fallen and broken a hip, the man who was trapped in his bathtub for three days, another who fell, while brushing his teeth, I believe, and got his hands trapped by his collapsing walker. I think he was rescued within a day or so. I remember all those whose lives stopped or were changed for good by a moment's failure of the heart or the brain, or by the carelessness of others.

But there's a deeper and more disturbing disjointedness of aging, something that both wounds us and isolates us. Not only do we come to an end, and all the things and people we love come to an end, but we meet those ends separately. Couples who've become one flesh by living together rarely can die together. The person who would have been most delighted with the books I've written would have been my mother, a great and constant reader. But she died twenty years before the first one was published. We've done funerals for parents who've died too young, bitterly lamenting they'd never see their children grow. On the other end of the scale, I have an elderly friend who's seen all her relatives and most of her contemporaries die, leaving her pretty much alone in the world.

We say sometimes that part of the preciousness of the things we treasure is in their transience, their mortality. I've said it once or twice myself in funeral sermons. It's the beauty of flowers; I suppose that's why they seem so natural at funerals. But is that really why they're precious and loved? I'd just as soon flowers could hang around a little longer and not be bulldozed or covered with concrete or withered by winter or withered by only age. We go to great lengths to preserve works of art. No one thinks Renaissance art is less precious because it's lasted for centuries. And how about our beautiful, fragile earth? I'd just as soon human stupidity and greed weren't destroying it. It's becoming more lethal, not more lovable, as we're warping its life. Praising the beauty of the transient seems like one more human act of self-deception, one more way we hide from what we can't order or control.

It's our endings being both known and unknown that unnerves us and unsettles us, I think. Our last years have a weird kind of formlessness: the ending is absolutely certain, its nearness increases every day, yet the how of it and the when of it are absolutely unknown. I've sometimes wondered if it would bring us peace to know our specific day of death and the way it would come to us, or if that would only give us something else to rage against. As it is, our path to wisdom and peace lies in accepting how circumscribed we are, how helplessly out of step with our loves and desires, how dark our vision, how satisfied we must be in our limits. I'm reminded of something John von Neumann once said about math but I've always thought could be said about life itself: we never really understand anything; we just get used to it.

III

One Sunday, during our church's coffee hour, I found myself standing with a few other retired people, chatting about their bucket lists. (For the uninitiated, a bucket list is a list of things you'd really like to do before you kick the bucket, i.e., die. Realistically, however, since these lists usually involve action, travel, or greater than ordinary exertion, they also need to be done before your body fails you too severely or you're confined to a nursing home. Maybe we should call them bed pan lists.). As I recall, most of the people talked mainly about places they'd still like to visit. Finally, someone, probably noticing my profound disinterest, looked at me and said, "So how about you? What's on your list?"

Without a thought, I blurted out, "I just want this comedy to be over."

That pretty much finished the conversation. I admit my answer surprised me as much as it surprised anybody. It's a moment I've since considered just as revelatory as my fight with my mother's ghost. But I'm not exactly sure what it revealed about me.

I don't remember feeling particularly hopeless or exhausted or depressed or fed up that morning. I didn't speak angrily or dismissively: I seemed to myself to be stating a fairly neutral fact. There simply wasn't anything I was yearning to do before my end.

Turning this incident over in my mind, I've wondered if it revealed some deep sense of peace with my life, or some helpless judgment of the smallness of all things human, or a satisfied acceptance of what I've done and seen. (I could, justifiably or not, see these things flowing out of a kind of Christian freedom from the fever of life.) I've wondered, too, if it had something to do with always being wrapped up in my calling, allowing it to define me: done with that, I'm done with all.

It's easy for me to find things to do, but there's nothing that's eating at me to be done. There's nothing I'm afraid I'll miss. My study continues to fill up with manuscripts and drawings, as my computer fills up with photographs. But it no longer seems important that any of it gets finished, or even preserved. I do seem to have an irrational feeling of being finished with everything already.

Something I've always found inspiring was Shakespeare's decision, at the end of his career, to simply leave the theatre and go home, not even bothering to arrange for those marvelous plays to be published or seeming to worry much about how the world remembered him. That probably reveals a certain amount of peace and satisfaction, a certain judgment about the place of human things. And I suppose you could see that flowing out of a kind of artistic freedom from the fever of life.

Still, all that said, I have also looked back on my spontaneous confession and wondered if I've been fooling myself about it, that it really did reveal a deep and unconscious hopelessness or exhaustion or depression or disgust. I'm not sure how you rise above mood and moment to make a reasonable conclusion about that.

However, if the making and keeping of bucket lists implies a certain amount of energy, I would have to admit that as I age I do struggle with the loss or the lack of energy. Each morning, as I wake up and sit on the side of my bed, I face some of my accusers. Almost every room in our house is lined with book shelves, but the two beside my bed hold the literature of the nineteenth century, from a complete set of the Waverley novels on my left to Tolstoy and Dostoevsky at eye-level as I sit there, along with hefty volumes like *Middlemarch, Moby Dick, With Fire and Sword, Germinal*, a set of Balzac, and a set of Dickens. I've read almost all of them and they wait there to be revisited. Each morning I stare at them and I think: How? How? How did I read all these books? When did I find the time? Where did I get the energy? And this was while I was serving as a pastor! And these two bookshelves are only two of many! I once read easily past midnight; now I'm euphoric if I don't nod off before ten. I marvel at how long it takes me to do anything, and how tired it leaves me.

Some days I think the most sensible thing I do is sleep. It's no longer hard to imagine a time when, like my parishioner Kay, I would do little else. There are days I wake up and remark to Mary Carol, "Maybe I can take a nice nap this afternoon." It gets me a laugh, and I'm only half serious. But I am at least half serious, and I've learned to take that nap if I want to keep functioning in the evening.

This is probably only the outcry of a driven person, whose body isn't willing to come along for the ride anymore. The wise person, no doubt, would simply smile and settle for what's left.

I happened, a while back, to acquire a book on aging by an author I admire very much. I opened it at random one day and found a passage of such dauntless perkiness that I slammed the book shut and haven't opened it since. No doubt unfairly, I decided writers who praise the glories of aging had probably been cheerleaders in high school, then civic boosters, always waving fistfuls of raffle tickets, perhaps even working as motivational speakers, ready to ridicule your weakness and bark at your failures.

My natural tendency is very much in the opposite direction, at times destructively so. From time to time during my church service, I seemed to exist in a cloud of hopelessness, or in a dark sealed room, where I could see no way ahead. I would get through it with my rituals and my routines (and I'll note it's useful to have a lifetime of discipline to draw on): get out of bed, clean up, get dressed, tie your shoes, make the bed. There are mornings when that sequence still comes in handy, though it's cut short now because I can't continue: go to the office, check for messages, check the calendar, start the day's list, etc. In fact, there are mornings when I gasp at how little I have to do. After a lifetime of days filled with tasks I could never complete, it's easy to feel pointless.

But the small hours of the night are the worst, the nights when I wake from some nightmare, or only some worry, some agitation enough to keep sleep from returning, and I lie there again in that cloud of hopelessness, that dark sealed room, choking on every problem I'll never solve, every injury and illness that will never heal, every word, every act, every mistake, every hurt I can never mend and never forget. If I've sent off a note the day before I meant as funny, I'm sure now it was disastrously insulting. If I finished some writing or drawing the day before, it's all I can do to keep myself from rising and destroying it.

It helps, then, that depression is a very old friend, whose ways I've long known, and I've learned to remind myself that the early hours always bring these thoughts to me, that they usually pass in the morning, that there will be time then to mend the hurts I imagine I've given, to destroy or to keep the last day's work.

The worst nights—so far—came when we were finally working on our will, thinking about powers of attorney, advance directives, the possible need of long-term care, and sorting out the mountain of possessions we've piled up around us, thinking, too, about what it would be like to live alone. During one of those bleak hours, I thought Mary Carol had stopped breathing. After I held my own breath, listening for hers, and knew she hadn't, it came to me that I had little idea, where we live now, of how the emergency services worked, beyond dialing 911 and telling my story. In the small towns of Minnesota that we served in, I knew the sheriffs, the town cops, the coroner, all the funeral directors, and a good number of the hospital personnel. We had first responders that attended our churches. In one of the towns, I served on the ambulance board and knew the EMTs. I have nothing close to that personal network here. In that particular dark night of the soul, I felt a chilling isolation around me, a cold emptiness, stretching far beyond my sight or reach.

Some of those nights, I prayed—I'm not sure how seriously—that I might die before dawn. On the very worst of those nights, I tried to think of a sure and painless way I could end both our lives at the same time. (That I was looking for something sure and painless suggests I couldn't have been that serious. Anyway, I never thought of one.)

But then real dawn would show up: I'd see lights moving across the ceiling as my neighbor Steve backed out of his driveway to go to work, the birds sang, the newspaper plopped in our driveway, the dark lightened to gray, then lightened more, and all of it brought . . . well, enough hope to be going on with.

When I began this writing, I had planned to present, or imagined I could present, in this final section, some sort of settled view of death and life, living and dying. I might say that, in the writing, I found I wasn't sure what I thought; but it would be more accurate to say: I thought, think, lots of things. (This really doesn't surprise me. I've often thought someone should carve on my gravestone: "Yes, but . . ." or "On the other hand . . .")

I can look ahead, almost any morning, to the coming day with either (or both) of two warring visions: I can see a day that's full and meaningful, or a day that's empty and meaningless; I can wonder how I'll get through the hours until night, or how I'll manage to work in what I'm eager to do; I can look at ageing and see peace and serenity, or misery and loss.

The face of the world seems so thin to me now, the veil so easily parted. But the parting of the veil can reveal the flourishing of life, its radiant beauty, or it can reveal its corruption, its futility. The deepest disquiet that comes over me is not the uncertainty of ageing, or the undeniable end to it, but the sheer senselessness of it. The constant physical maintenance your body needs to age with health is a constant reminder of how much you're trying to fight off. Always beneath you is the threat of illness, accident, the ending. Beneath all the plans and goings on, the fundamental act of your life is waiting for the end. Again, continuing to live, fighting to continue to live, starts to seem absolutely senseless. It's hard not to ask: What's the point? Why all this work for the inevitable defeat? Why must it go on? Why can't we simply end? If that's hard not to ask, how easy is it to answer?

Sometimes I've joked: well, I'd still like to read more books, see more movies, have a few more servings of fettucine alfredo, with garlic bread, and drink a few more bottles of sauvignon blanc. (I suppose that might count as a primitive bucket list.). But how much of a joke is it? Some days I would be challenged to come up with something better. Certainly, I could concoct a more idealistic and noble-sounding list, but I'm not sure it would be more honest.

We could say that the old, we old ones, are, simply by our being here, a gift and a blessing to the young. We could point out the impoverishment and limited horizons of communities that lack an active elderly presence. We might remind ourselves of how much organizations and institutions lose when they lose the living vessels of institutional memory or shortsightedly rid themselves of them. I believe all those things. I'm sure I've said them in a sermon or two.

But do we need so many of us? Do we, to be blunt, need me? The ninety-year old former president, Jimmy Carter, still bringing his wisdom on world affairs, teaching Sunday school, still shopping at the dollar store, and helping build houses for Habitat for Humanity can be an inspiration for anybody. The seventy-year old Cordell Strug, sitting under a gingko tree with his dog, scribbling on one sheet of paper after another . . . not so much.

I don't have a Facebook account. It's one more way I hide from the world. But there were a couple of people I wanted to follow, so I created one for Yum-Yum. If you're on Facebook, you get notifications of the birthdays of your "friends" and a suggestion that you send them greetings. My usual greeting is something like: "Have a good one and keep the numbers climbing." Someone once, intriguingly, replied to my greeting with a question: "How high do the numbers go?"

My response was: "Some days: not high enough . . . other days: enough already."

IV

When Mary Carol and I were both rushing off in the evening to council meetings, committee meetings, confirmation classes, and study groups, the dishes would pile up through the week until it took a marathon washing session on the weekends to clear the counters and start over. Now that we've retired, we can wash each day's dishes immediately after supper and have an easy domestic ritual to end the day and begin the evening.

We switch off washing and drying. I was standing next to the dish drainer one night, waiting to begin drying, when I began to feel dizzy; I had that fuzzy head sensation and my vision started to narrow and the things in front of me seemed to be rushing away from me. I woke up on the floor with my glasses off somewhere, the dish drainer on my chest, and my foot twisted painfully sideways under the kitchen counter. Mary Carol was kneeling over me. She said, "What just happened?"

A few days later, I fainted again. That time, I fell against the kitchen table and managed to whack both my head and the base of my spine.

This little crisis had been on its way for a while. For a few months, I'd been having slight episodes of dizziness, when a buzzing wave would seem to sweep over my head, then recede. Usually, that was it, and I'd shrug and move on. But about a month before my two fainting spells, we were at the Art Institute when I had a more serious episode. We usually split up at the Art Institute and follow our own interests at our own pace. I was down in the American section and, luckily, I was fairly close to a corner. I started to feel my familiar head buzzing, but this time it was worse. I started to sway and braced myself against the corner. When the wave passed, I felt sick and drained and sought out some water and a quiet place to sit. I did wonder what would have happened if the spell had been worse and I had been in the city alone. Still, my response was to shrug again, move on, and hope for the best.

But the fainting, with the pretty solid blows to my head and spine, finally sent me into the world of medical care, and on the familiar journey of modern medicine: being sent from doctor to doctor and being put through every test (and every machine) scientific brilliance has devised. I took this journey, over the years, with many of my parishioners and saw a lot of the tours come up empty. Now it was my turn, and I must say I enjoyed meeting the doctors and I found the machines fascinating. It was fun comparing the different cultures of the offices: in one office, no matter when I'd visit, everyone seemed to be racing around, as though an emergency siren were constantly wailing; in another, the staff was so relaxed I feared they'd fall sleep and forget about me; some staffs chattered happily and joked with each other as they passed; others had furrowed brows, barely nodded to one another, and spoke little to me. Most of the tests did come up empty and I'm guessing that was no news to the doctors.

The weirdest test I had was a kind of elaborately staged brain scan. I had to fast from the night before and only sleep from midnight to five a.m. Then I had to report to the lab without washing my hair (or applying anything to it). They settled me in a lounging chair and stuck wires all over my head. The room was dark and chilly, so they covered me in a blanket, told me not to move, and hoped I'd fall asleep. Lights were flashing in different patterns and there were some noises I couldn't help thinking were whales crooning. Test results: normal.

The most helpful encounter I had was with a cardiologist, a dynamic character with the happy staff I mentioned above. After I told my story to the nurse, as always, I waited a bit. Then there was a sharp rap on the door, the doctor burst in, and proclaimed, "I know exactly what's wrong with you. I'm going to give you some simple things to do. You're going to laugh at them, and think I'm crazy, but, if you walk out of here and do what I tell you to do, you probably won't faint again." (He was right.) I was never more glad to meet that soaring medical arrogance that used to infuriate me but, at this particular moment, lifted my spirits.

The most thrilling adventure I had was with another cardiologist. He was concerned with some irregularities in my heartbeat, so concerned that he thought I should have a surgical procedure *the very next morning* where he could get a more detailed view of the problem and possibly install a pacemaker. He stressed the urgency and the danger of not addressing the problem, but I somehow failed to fully absorb that the surgical procedure involved stopping my heart. (Mary Carol really flipped when she belatedly learned of this.)

At the hospital, I seemed to myself to be fairly calm and at peace. After I was prepared, two very young people walked in the room to wheel my bed into surgery. I thought they were junior high nursing volunteers, but they turned out to be part of the surgical team. I'm proud to say I never once asked if they shouldn't find someone older to do this.

Almost three hours later, I came to as the team leader was pushing my bed back to my room. She wore a bright scarf around her head and she was smiling. I felt like I'd been kidnapped by a happy pirate. She said, "We couldn't accomplish very much because we could never get your heart to stop. And, believe me, we tried!"

In the waiting room, Mary Carol had a visit from the surgeon himself, telling her of yet another procedure they could do at yet another hospital. But finding out he'd meant to stop my heart made her see him as little better than a murderer.

The post-op nurses watching me were at first reluctant to let me go home. Though I thought I was calm and at peace, my blood pressure somehow climbed to a personal best (or worst, I guess) of 205/110. I waited for half an hour, then told them they couldn't keep me there if I wanted to leave, and I was going home. During the night, I had my final illumination: if a trained and determined surgical team couldn't stop my heart in almost three hours of trying, the stubborn little organ was unlikely to stop on its own. So I pulled the plug on all further tests, and that was the end of that particular medical journey.

But there were times, during it, when death seemed very close and fear, of incapacity and of loss, came upon us personally and intimately, with all its captivating power.

When I was having dizzy spells and fainting, not knowing when they'd come upon me or how bad they'd be, it was impossible to be blind to the danger of being out and about on my own, even for short trips to the library or the grocery store. Before this, one of my great pleasures had been taking the train into the city and wandering the streets at whim with my camera. It wasn't hard to imagine striking my head on a curb after falling or even dropping off the lakeside walk into Lake Michigan. My world quickly grew very small. One doctor told me, after fainting, I shouldn't drive for six months. After a couple of nervous trial runs, I more or less agreed with him and so had to be ferried everywhere.

More deeply troubling, however, was the fear of ultimate loss that came upon us as a long-married couple. This was especially sharp for Mary Carol, since her father had died fairly young of a heart attack. My habitual mask of calm and flippant bravado probably didn't help much. When we did premarital counseling, we always told young couples they really would become one flesh. They would *live together*, not just cohabit or share the same space and time. All they did as the years went by would more and more be the acts of the one new creature they became together. They would, as we came to do, work through the tasks of the day almost without thought or discussion. They would cover for each other, clean up after each other, examine each other's wounds, remind each other about keeping appointments or taking meds. So: when your partner dies, you lose half your life. Or, more strongly: half of every part of it.

I asked Mary Carol if she thought all married people hoped they'd die before their partners. She said she was sure of it.

On some of those bleak nights I spoke of, I've turned over in my mind which desire might be more selfish: to die first or die last, to be the one to go or the one to stay. It's probably an unanswerable question, especially if you want to answer it without illusions or posturing. But it's probably unanswerable mainly because you aren't you alone any longer. You're mainly thinking of the loss: not wanting to lose the other.

Fear of being trapped, fear of being alone: these strike at the heart of our nature, our living: losing our activity, losing our bonds.

We attended a weekly church group around this time, which was led by another retired pastor in our church, Pastor Robert. (I often feel sorry for our young pastors, looking out from the pulpit each week at four or five grumpy retired pastors.). The group was a kind of combination devotion-study group and managed to be a fairly illuminating and inspiring session, week by week, with prayer, time for silence, exploring of texts, and sharply focused discussions. One week, Pastor Robert asked us, mostly elderly, mostly attending in couples, what we feared the most. We might as well have drawn lots to choose one person at random to speak for everyone; we all feared the loss of the powers and the connections that allowed us to attend that morning session and to do everything else we did. We feared incapacity, weakness, the lessening of our powers. One quite elderly person lived with his son, who had been seriously injured in a car accident. He said he feared dying and leaving him alone, though his brothers loved and would care for him. He feared losing his power to help. I saw in that another form of the spouse's fear of a life together being gone.

As I sat there listening to the different yet nearly identical fears, I thought they came to us so readily because they struck at our nature as creatures, our very physical reality: we fear, at bottom, losing our access to space and our access to time. We fear losing light and order. We fear our world falling back into chaos, with the unravelling and dissolving beginning inside us.

I should put that in more physical terms.

I flesh out the fears for myself with all the knowledge of helplessness and vulnerability I've gathered over the years. I still sometimes wince when I think of the injuries I've seen; I've put up my arm to deflect imaginary blows. Remembering broken bodies, I can feel so brittle I'm afraid I'll shatter if I trip and fall.

Nursing homes taught me too much about the wreckage of the flesh: losing your sight, losing your hearing, being so physically severed from everything that you scream if someone touches you, losing the movement of your fingers, your hands, arms, legs, losing the limbs themselves, wearing a diaper because you can't crawl to the bathroom, your hands shaking so much most of your food spills down your clothes until they realize you have to be fed by someone else, if they ever do, pissing yourself and shitting yourself because no one answered your buzzer, even if you managed to reach it, then having to lie in your own waste until you're cleaned up by aides who want to scream in frustration because there are too few of them and too much shit.

I have a friend who knows as much about the wounding and the decay of bodies as I do: he's made his children promise to kill him before the worst happens to him. We might at least all agree that, at some point, death really can be welcomed as a friend.

One of our seminary professors remarked once that older societies feared sudden death because it would deny the time to say farewell, to settle affairs, to reach out in repentance or forgiveness or simply in friendship and love one last time. We moderns, he noted, wish for the sudden death they feared, to spare ourselves.

But it's the helpless lingering we fear, the enforced, trapped lingering that only we moderns can experience. The power of our medical care that heals and keeps us healthy can also keep us living in helplessness. It's death's shadow, that shrinks and darkens our lives, not death itself, that terrifies us most.

V

Looking back on the class where we shared our fears, it surprises me a little that no one brought up the fear of dementia, losing the powers of the mind, losing our understanding of the world, feeling our very self erode and slowly vanish, blurring like a fading picture. We all spoke of lingering in physical helplessness, but dementia can come upon the physically healthy and active and leave them lost in a different, sadder kind of lingering.

One of my grandmothers became confused and haunted in her final years, but I was young then and probably thought her condition was something that commonly happened to the very old. The first time I was really confronted with someone who had fallen out of our world into some other and stranger life was fairly early in my ministry. I had served for a few months as a vice-pastor for a nearby church whose pastor had moved, and I came to know some of the church leaders fairly well. A year or two later, I was surprised to run into one of them, restrained in a wheelchair, at one of the local nursing homes. I assumed he'd had an accident or a stroke because I'd known him as a big, vibrant guy, not that old, one of those physically imposing natural leaders you like having on a church council. I went up to him, offered my hand, and said, "Hi, Bob. What's got you in here?"

He looked up at me slowly. His face seemed both uncomprehending and disgusted. Then he said, "You son of a bitch. You think you're so fucking smart. Well, you don't know shit."

I stood there frozen, staring at him. I must have looked stunned and helpless because one of the nurses came over and led me away from him. "He doesn't know who you are," she said. "He doesn't know where he is or what he's saying."

But I seemed to myself like the one who didn't know anything. It was almost impossible not to take the familiar face and the familiar voice as the familiar man I knew, who was finally telling me what he thought of me. It was hard not to feel rattled, assaulted, sick, and humiliated. I felt the frightening fragility of the world of meaning we create together and how easily and completely someone can fall out of it. This has to be one of the most bewildering and wounding things for a spouse or a child of someone stricken like that to go through.

As the years went by, I no longer encountered dementia as a sudden, frightening shock, and rarely saw it in so violent a form; I saw it come upon those I knew slowly, one small lapse, one momentary confusion, one failure of memory, of awareness, after another. You share the early jokes about memory being good but short, you shake your heads together about senior moments. Then you realize the person you've known so long is fully present before you less and less. You're watching them fade, disappear, hollow out from within, and you're watching your life, the life you've known together, hollow out with them.

You can watch this a lot if you're a regular member of a church congregation.

At the last church we served, one of our members was a retired school administrator, an intelligent and genial man, always nattily dressed. One Thursday, he wandered into the office and asked when the (Sunday) service would start and why there were so few cars in the parking lot. We laughed a bit about getting days mixed up, but this happened more than once. He began to look more and more rumpled. People started seeing him parked in his car on some of the less travelled country roads, with no idea where he was or where he was going. Finally, he couldn't be allowed to drive and, soon, couldn't be allowed to live on his own.

The church we became members of when we retired, about ten years ago, was, and still is, a pretty lively place, with lots of bright, active people. I've watched three of the brightest, most active of them slowly fade out of our common life. Still physically healthy, still accompanying their spouses on Sundays, they've spoken less and less or made less and less sense or told the same stories and asked the same questions in ever smaller cycles of repetition or simply stood among us, waiting to be led through the day.

I was shaken one day when a quirky woman with a sharp wit, standing next to me, asked her spouse, "Where are we exactly?"

All the spouses bear up and I'm awed by how indomitable they are in maintaining their life in the community. But it has to be a lonely task, a frustrating and exhausting task, and there must be a sea of sorrow wearing away at them.

I've spent a lifetime looking for direction and hope for hopeless times in passages of the Bible and what came to me as I was brooding about dementia was Luke's set of parables about the lost: lost sheep, lost coin, lost (better known as prodigal) son. At least the sheep and the son are widely known, and they are defining images of Christian life and the Christian understanding of God. Each portrays the unstoppable search for the lost one and, in the son's case, the unquestioned (and foolish seeming) welcome and restoration. The interesting question from our side of things is: do the lost ones know they're lost? The son does but you could argue fairly pointedly that what he really knows is his misery. The sheep may or may not know it's lost: that's made it a good and powerful image of the sinner. Whatever the sheep (or anyone else) thinks, it belongs to the flock and the shepherd's going to keep chasing after it.

But, for my purposes here, the parable between these two is the intriguing one: the lost coin. A woman loses a coin. She lights up and sweeps the house, searches until she finds it, then celebrates with her neighbors the way the angels do when a sinner repents. But the coin doesn't repent: it's just found. The coin *can't* know it's lost. It can't even know it belonged to the woman. This parable is the most absolute about the claim, the care, and the action of God, whether we're aware of anything or not.

That's not only hope for the sinner or for the sinner blind to sin but for all the lost, *no matter how they're lost*. Even if they can't recognize themselves, God can and God will care for them and come for them. That's a proclamation I can easily see myself making in a funeral sermon.

But if you push the point, as you should, and ask why a kind, caring, and watchful power would let us get so lost in the first place, I don't have an answer that satisfies me, and neither does anyone else.

But I wonder if the loss of awareness, the loss of memory and of recognition, the inability to know our condition, the isolation dementia brings, reducing us to something like the lost coin, might not suggest an answer to the question I began with: when my study group discussed its fears of aging, why didn't dementia loom larger?

I think it's hard for most of us to imagine ignorance or unconsciousness. Try imagining knowing less than you do (or more than you do, for that matter). The state of our consciousness is the center-point of our world circle, our anchor in life, and it's virtually set in concrete. I can imagine fainting again, and waking up from fainting, but lying unconscious is literally beyond me.

So while we can easily imagine and fear pain, crippling wounds, physical failure, it's hard to imagine, and thus to fear, our own minds darkening, losing knowledge of the obvious and well-known, being disconnected from everything around us. It's something we see happening to others, so we can fear its coming upon others, upon those we know and care about. That makes it easy to see dementia as something that *only* happens to others, easy to refuse out of hand the knowledge that it can happen to all.

It's easier to dismiss as a personal threat, and I think that's why it wasn't really much of a part of our class discussion. But it's not an impossible fear to acquire.

We usually take Yum-Yum on her last walk shortly before we go to bed. Before that, I'm usually upstairs reading and Mary Carol is downstairs sewing or working on quilts. When the time comes, we call to each other, meet on the landing, and out we go.

One night, Mary Carol called up the steps that it was time. I was a little annoyed with myself for nodding off (again) over my book. Still perhaps a little sleepy, I walked down the steps and saw Mary Carol putting on her coat. Yum-Yum was already at the door, scoping out the yard.

Then I noticed the light was still on downstairs. I turned to the person putting her coat on whom I somehow no longer saw as Mary Carol. She seemed to be a stranger yet her presence there seemed not to puzzle me at all. What puzzled me was Mary Carol being, to my lost mind, still downstairs.

I remember how confused I felt. I turned to the person standing next to me, and I said, "So . . . where's Mary Carol?"

The stranger answered, "I'm right here."

My head seemed to clear, I recognized her, and said hurriedly, "Yeah. Okay. So we're ready, right?"

Was I just not quite awake yet? Was this a momentary lapse or an early warning sign?

It's one more time to shrug and move on, one more thing I'll be waiting to find out.

But it did give me a little jolt.

VI

Our youngest grandson, Martin, has an observant eye and a sharp wit. Being in a gathering with him is what it must have been like to be at a party with Dorothy Parker or Virginia Woolf. You can see him taking mental notes and sharpening his darts. He's always primed with jokes and stories. Here's one I'm still chuckling about:

Martin: "I invented a new word but you're not going to believe me."
Me: "What's the word?"
Martin: "Plagiarism."

Assuming he got this from somebody else, I'm still impressed a junior high student would appreciate it enough to use it himself to get a laugh.

A few months ago, when I was at lunch with him and our son Jon, he gave me the question I'm going to use to end this writing. It was a problem he set for us: "What would you do if you knew you only had one day to live?"

I said, "Do you mean the end of the world? Or just you personally are going to die tomorrow?"

"Just you."

"And you're sure?"

"Yes."

I don't recall that either Jon or I had a ready answer, but Martin didn't wait very long. "Here's what I'd do: I'd rob fifty armored cars and, when the cops came to get me, I'd say: 'What are you going to do? Drag my lifeless body into court?'"

He was clearly less interested in the money than in using the killer exit-line he had come up with. I foresee a career in the arts for him.

But to address our question: what *would* I do if I knew I had only one day to live? Sitting in the booth with Martin and Jon, my first thought was of books I might want to re-read: *Hamlet* and *Finnegans Wake* floated through my mind. But then I got a strong image, another of those unplanned, instinctive responses that seem to reveal something deeper than thought: thinking of reading, I saw myself not reading, but looking up from whatever unimportant thing was in my lap, looking up from my familiar seat under the gingko tree, with Yum-Yum lying on the other side, looking out at the dog walkers and up at the clouds. I thought of a phrase I found in Hannah Arendt's *Life of the Mind* that I always liked: "the sheer entertainment value of the world," all the many things it offers to see, hear, smell, and touch. So I guess that's my answer: I'd sit under my gingko and let creation entertain me one last time.

I'm coming to the end of this writing in Advent, my favorite season of the church year. I like the way the Advent readings gather up the hopes and dreams of centuries, the small signs appearing in the most unexpected places, the waiting people who aren't always sure what they're waiting for, and shape them all into a story looking beyond itself. I've always been happier in the meditative seasons of Advent and Lent, which don't really lend themselves to the trumpets and drums of Christian triumph which we deploy on our major festivals. Theologians are fond of saying the Christian victory, the arrival of God's kingdom, is "already, not yet." But, most of the time, to those of us at ground level, "not yet" seems a lot more accurate than "already." So the trumpets and drums always seem a little premature.

When I taught the liturgical year, I used to say that each season had its characteristic spirituality, its unique vision and mood, but that every season, always, was a necessary part of the fullness of Christian spirituality. Still, I've loved most the quiet waiting of Advent and maybe as well the hints of melancholy in some of the stories and hymns, as though some part of us isn't all that sure we're up to whatever's coming.

Advent seems an appropriate time and place of the spirit for my ending, in every sense.

There's a mysterious but important thread in the story of Jesus told by the gospels: he's always seeking out lonely or deserted places where he can be by himself to pray. It's an easy thread for busy and active Christians of every sort to overlook. But from the first chapter of Mark, the earliest gospel, Jesus goes off, after a burst of activity, to be alone. He never even announces he's about to disappear; it's as though he's driven, as the Spirit drove him into the wilderness, driven to regain something he's in danger of losing. And, from that first moment, someone immediately pursues him to bring him back to the crowd. Some translations bluntly state that the disciples "hunted" for him. (Every introvert will recognize that moment.) But Jesus keeps at it, up to the moment he's arrested. Even the famous scene of his walking on water comes about because he's been off alone.

We're usually not told what he prayed for or thought about it. That seems unremarkable—if he's praying alone, who would know?—until we reflect that all the evangelists are more than eager to fill in the blanks elsewhere. But the habitual prayer of Jesus mostly remains a mystery, suggesting the mystery of the world his spirit dwells in, both in and beyond ours, suggesting, too, a realm beyond words that he needs to sustain him.

His relentless flight from the actions, the talking, the crowds, his fight to be alone, and our ignorance of what he's about there also give him a kind of loneliness. It occurs to me that this can provide another way to see the cross as a strange fulfillment of his strange life.

I always found this side of Jesus very attractive, as all the quietists, contemplatives, and mystics of Christian history have. There were times, both during my church service and during the years of the civil rights and anti-war movements, when it seemed a lifeline to me, an offering of a place beyond angry crowds and endless meetings. I would in no sense consider myself a mystic but another thing I used to say, in my teaching days, was that the mystics, like the martyrs and the missionaries, should be part of every Christian's landscape. We don't all have to be, or aspire to be, any of those, but they should all be on the horizon of our possibilities.

But, again, the mystics, the contemplatives, were those I was most drawn to, their sense of being slightly apart from everything yet completely wrapped up in it all. I wrote my dissertation on William James's *Varieties of Religious Experience* and Thomas Merton is still one of the authors I return to. Now that my days are filling up with silence and solitude, I feel I'm completing another circle of my life, becoming more myself, or a self I'm more comfortable with. You might, as an ending, imagine me on my last day, sitting and contemplating things one last time.

In the final pages of his *Tractatus*, the philosopher Ludwig Wittgenstein, who was a kind of mystic without transcendence, makes an interesting remark about death: that it's not an event in life and that our life really has no end, in the way our visual field has no limits. I once took him as making the obvious point that our death is an experience for others, not for us, but he's really pointing to something more: that our living, in some essential way, excludes death; however natural a process it is, it remains unnatural to our experience. This would be as true for others watching us die as for us dying. I think he was getting at something like the oddness I talked about in my introduction, when it felt weird and almost rude to walk out of Kay's room after she'd stopped breathing.

So I would say, along this line, that there's really no natural way to end this writing. The ending is beyond me, in every sense.

To speak of the ending, not of this writing but of my life, in a very practical sense it will belong not to me but to others. (In one of my notes for this section, I find this: "finally a death when I don't have to say anything!").

Someone else will preside at the rite and shape the sermon. If I die slowly enough, someone else will have to sit and watch and listen for my last breath.

I said, in my introduction, that my life has been one of those that give pastors an easy time in funeral sermons: reasonably full of the ordinary satisfactions that most people can understand and that many people would give anything to have had: a good number of years, health, work, children, grandchildren. But much of my lucky and privileged life seems like something that just happened to me, that didn't have that much to do with me, and even, at times, like something that happened to somebody else.

I identify my life more with my adventures in art and scholarship: things I wrote, things I drew or photographed, classes I led, choirs I sang in, plays I acted in, sermons I delivered. I'm far less sociable than many of the people I wrote about and far less wrapped up in the satisfactions I celebrated for them. My satisfaction came more from writing about them and trying to get it right; that was one of the things that my years allowed me to do.

I can't work up a lot of interest in anything that would count as a life after this one. I'd settle for dissolving back into the cosmic mix. Since most of our conceptions of an afterlife seem to involve the endurance of our consciousness, it strikes me as one more monument to human self-importance. Even when we try to imagine a world without us, we imagine ourselves watching it. In our religious thought, of course, we also imagine watching all the scores being settled. Since it's clear that in this world the wicked prosper and the righteous don't, it's natural and nice to think a time might come when things would be otherwise. Certainly, the stories and parables of Jesus contain visions like that. What they don't contain, or at least what I can't see in them, is much of a picture of that other life in that other time. Most of what he says about judgment and about what the kingdom of God is like bears on this life more than any other, on what's at work in this life and how we are to live in it.

Some theologian I read long ago—I think it was H. Richard Niebuhr—said that we like to think the most fundamental question is: what should I do?, but that there's a deeper, prior one: what's going on? Clearly there's truth to that: we act out of our understanding. And yet just what is going on, in the largest sense, is what we've all been arguing about since humans learned to argue. We can almost be defined by the argument.

What Christians say is going on is part of the argument and certainly provides an understanding out of which we can act. But, as with the parables of Jesus, it's less a clear and detailed picture of what reality is than a direction and a guide for us within whatever it is, a flickering light for whatever dark path we're on.

But it's time for me to come up with whatever's going to serve as the ending of this.

It's still Advent, only a week before Christmas. Even Yum-Yum's beginning to find the low temperatures and the harsh winds a bit much for extended sessions under our gingko tree. But there are still days when she trots out happily to her watching post and I follow her, my feet crunching now on the frozen grass, all the leaves gone, the bushes brown, and here and there some traces of snow from the little we've had. I cringe a little when I lower myself to the frozen metal bench, but it's been nice to be there over the years as the seasons change.

We can, of course, be out there so far into the winter because our fragile and battered planet is in a catastrophic spiral of violent climate change, bringing ever-new unforeseen consequences that the dire warnings and reports can hardly keep up with. People walk by us and shout "Beautiful day!," apparently unconcerned that our grandchildren will be living a nightmare in a few decades. It's hard to be peacefully entertained by creation when you know how much damage we've done to it.

One of the gloomier reports I've read recently bears on my reflections in this final section. The writer noted that we've hardly begun exploring the havoc climate change will bring to the world's food supply, how much we'll be able to produce but, further, how much nutritional value it will have. But then he reflected on the spiritual impact this might have on us: we've lived toward death and change before, but always with the blind assumption that people much like us would follow us and care about things at least similar to those we care about: what if we could no longer assume we'd be followed by anybody or by anybody living a life we would recognize? What would that do to our projects, to anything we'd invest in or leave behind?

Clearly, the suggestion was: it would take the heart out of everything we did. Any hollowness or futility we felt about our ending would only grow deeper and darker. So: how would you answer my grandson Martin's question in this more extreme case: what would you do if you knew the entire human story would end tomorrow?

Or would it really change things? Many others before us have been sure the world would end, and, while for some of them it did mean complete collapse, others carried on, to be vindicated by time and the unknown future. Religion is usually blamed for those baseless fears, and we might appeal today to some accurate and undeniable scientific evidence of doom. But even our secular fears have often been fueled by mythic categories, apocalyptic nightmares that come from something within us other than reason and observation. I would note too that the response we actually see today in people absorbing such reports and warnings is that more of them are fighting to do something about it.

That seems like a fairly recognizable human response to me. So here I am scribbling down my reflections, still assuming someone like me might find something in them someday.

But now it really is time to bring to an end at least this part of me.

I had originally planned to do my own version of Prospero's abandonment of his magic. Something like:

All my rough labors I here abjure. I'll snap my pencils, unplug my computer, take the battery out of my camera, gather up my pens and ink bottles, and bury them all in the earth. I'll drown my books in Lake Michigan (or at least put them in the hands of other readers). I'll still the tongue, still the mind and the heart. I'll gaze at creation's pageant. I'll breathe. (The end.)

But, honestly, I'm still too driven for that to happen anytime soon.

So I'll adapt another character in another story for my ending, one that has deeper roots in me.

There's a story in Mark's gospel that acts as a kind of hinge. Jesus is mostly through with all his arguments, his miracles, his lessons, and his travels; the story is about to leave the public arena and move toward the Passion. But, first, Jesus sits down and watches the human show. It's his last look at the folks before the fury of the crucifixion swallows and changes everything. He's sitting by the temple treasury and he's watching the offering. For once, he's observing instead of being the center of the action. The rich put in much, a widow puts in two small coins. Jesus famously praises the widow as giving the most, for she gave all she had.

(Luke tells the same story in the same sequence of events but he omits the detail of Jesus sitting down. In Luke, the observation on the widow becomes one more remark in a series of judgments, and the scene doesn't have the same weight of a full stop for a summing up that it has in Mark.)

But what intrigues me is what comes next. One of the disciples, probably hoping for a pat on the head, bids Jesus to admire the impressive look of that temple he just praised the widow for contributing to. But Jesus scoffs, as always, at earthly grandeur, religious or otherwise, and delivers the equally famous judgment that not one of the great stones will be left upon another. All will be in ruins.

It's the pairing of the two moments that strikes the spark of inspiration: Jesus, as he's departing from public life, praises one person's act of all-consuming devotion . . . to a doomed institution he refuses to admire.

There was more than one moment in my church service when I found that story absolutely inspiring, a bracing summons to persevere with no thought for reward or success. It seems to me not a bad beacon of light for life on earth, for me now, and for us all now.

There's one more thing to notice about the story. The widow is unnamed. She's like all the other unnamed people who encounter Jesus, who are lit up for a moment by the gospel, used by the gospel to light up something for us.

Then the light moves on and they disappear.

Brief Epilogue in Time of Plague

Not long after I finished the last chapter in the season of Advent, the novel coronavirus began its spread around the world. Before we were halfway through that other meditative season of the church year, Lent, hospitals were being overwhelmed with cases and the death toll was steadily rising. Soon all large gatherings and non-essential errands were banned, restaurants, theatres, parks, and churches were closed, and we, especially the elderly and vulnerable, were told to shelter in place. For the first time in my life, I attended Easter worship via a computer screen.

But, as readers of the last few chapters might guess, apart from the above restrictions, my hermit-like daily life didn't change that much. Most of what I work at now I work at alone, and I have no trouble filling my days. I do miss gathering with the church, as well as my other social contacts, which seem more numerous and vital now that I'm banned from them. But, considering the deprivation and misery this virus has brought to so many, I have neither reason nor right to complain about anything.

In fact, once again, what our changed life has shown me most vividly is the sheer luck of my being born when and where I was. Being a baby boomer, I missed the Spanish Flu, the Great Depression, and World War II. I was among the first children to receive the polio vaccine. When this new plague arrived, I had already been retired for years so I didn't have to face threats or challenges to my employment. I noted, in my introduction, that an African-American child who grew up just a few blocks away from me in Chicago would have had nothing like the resources and opportunities I had. That same child today would be far more vulnerable to illness and a shrinking economy and would be far more likely to die of COVID-19.

Some of the people who knew I was writing this book dropped me notes suggesting, or expressing assurance, that I would discuss the virus and what it had brought upon us. It wasn't something that had occurred to me or that I saw as in any way necessary. For one thing, I saw this writing as very much a picture of one life in one place and time. Also, I didn't think anything I'd said was in need of rewriting or qualification, simply because a new virus was sweeping the earth. I must admit, too, that I'd always been impatient with claims that whatever was happening to us was more devastating or more enriching, more senseless or more sensible, more frightening or more promising, than anything else anyone had ever gone through. I think people should be forced to read a lot more history than they seem to, so they might have at least a chance at some perspective. It might cushion the shock of discovering again, dismally, that things we can't see and don't think about can destroy us. It might provide them a few bracing comparisons. By the time I was getting these suggestions, I was getting sick of hearing the word "unprecedented."

All that said, here are my thoughts on life during the outbreak.

The morning I began this epilogue, one of the columnists I read in our daily newspaper spoke of the Day Everything Changed [his caps], referring, not to the invention of the printing press, not to the splitting of the atom, but to the last day he spent at his office desk several months ago. One often heard some version of "We've never been through anything like this." The "we" in that statement begs to be interrogated; it's clearly spoken by the voice of privilege. It's most clearly not the voice of the entire human race. All the shock and wonder, the gasping at the ever-climbing death toll, comes out of a privileged place and time, spared the waves of disease, the great plagues, the chronic pain and infection, and the short, perilous lifespans most of our ancestors had to contend with.

But, no doubt inevitably, I was most disturbed by comments I heard made by two pastors. All the news outlets have been continually speaking with those affected by the virus in any way and, one night, I heard interviews with two pastors who had been infected, both at or near retirement age. I wondered if the reporters underlined their mutual calling because they thought it gave more power to their testimony. The two men split neatly into one objective and one subjective outcry. One soberly confessed that it was the first time in his life that he found himself doubting the justice of life and the providence of God. The other spoke that simple, common, helpless protest: why did this happen to me?

I sat there at my kitchen table and, I suppose, went through my own version of shock and wonder at something I already should have known. But, still, how do you get to be sixty years old without noticing the injustice and senselessness of the world? How do you get out of high school without grasping that people might not deserve the miseries that get handed to them? How do you serve *as pastors* and never see anything that makes you question the justice of life and the providence of God? How do you never see anyone suffering without any reason? How does it not occur to you that someday it might be you? "Why me?" Why anyone? Why *not* you? I thought this was a pathetic failure of pastoral witness.

Consider that fundamental Christian image that should teach believers about death and life: Jesus the healer and teacher being tortured and dying slowly on a criminal's cross. Does that death make any sense to you? Why should your own?

I think we would gain in strength and compassion by thinking less about how different, unprecedented, or unique our situation is and more about what we have in common with those who have lived and suffered before us.

I began reading, soon after we started sheltering in place, Daniel Defoe's *A Journal of the Plague Year*, which presents itself as a survivor's account of the London plague of 1664–1665. Defoe's unadorned, journalistic style, chronicling random incidents and punctuated by statistical tables, creates the illusion of a contemporary document, but it also lets the reality of the plague, its silent coming and hidden spread, its relentless growth, be the real story. The parallels with our outbreak really are striking. There's the same slow grasp of how bad things are and might become. There's the same variety of human response: dismissal, fear and flight, determination, sacrifice, desperation and suspicion. There are strategies of distancing and isolation: infected people might be sealed in their houses, with guards outside to prevent their leaving. There's the same snow-balling economic collapse. Defoe sets down a stunning two-page list, vividly charting how the slowing of social activity and the measures taken against the plague eliminate the need for one group of workers after another, leaving them destitute and helpless. To Defoe's credit, he counts the cost of the plague in the misery of the poor.

As anyone familiar with Shakespeare's theatre knows, this wasn't the first plague to visit London, but its toll was high: something like 68 to 100,000 deaths out of a population of 460,000. (Then as now, accurate counting of the dead is difficult. "Probably higher" is a phrase still being used when we report our own numbers.) For another comparison, the Black Death of 1350 is said to have killed somewhere between 75 to 200 million, around 30 to 40 percent of Europe's population at the time.

I don't mean to minimize the devastation and the grief the virus has brought us, or how ghastly a disease it is. But I think it's strengthening to remind ourselves the world has been swept by plagues before, with immense losses. People like us have suffered from and fought against them; people like us have survived them and rebuilt their lives.

The peculiar anguish that a contagion brings is in the isolation and separation needed to control the outbreak. (Again, I'll underline this is not unique to our situation. Defoe chronicles isolation measures that are harsher and more extreme than ours. He also notes the fear that makes people flee each other without being ordered to.) But this does bring a spiritual wound. In the wake of other tragedies, our most fundamental response, sometimes our only possible response, is to come together and cling together. Much of what I've written in this book testifies to our need to be close and the power it brings us. More deeply, that need and that power derive from our physical yearning for each other and the sheer goodness of being together through all the times of our lives. It's the gift that comes with everything we do, and it's the very thing our isolating ourselves from each other deprives us of: all the gatherings of love, joy, celebration, and pleasure.

When our church buildings closed, there were, of course, plenty of voices to remind us "the church is not a building." (I hear that Sunday school jingle in my head as I write.). Yet staring at worship services on a computer screen for months ought to convince all but the most obtuse that, while the church is not a building, the building brings its own witness and is something we treasure for the acts done in its dedicated spaces and for the memories that hover all through it. Furthermore, as all in the church know, the punchline of that Sunday school jingle is "the church is the people," and we were denied the buildings precisely because we were first denied the gatherings of the people.

The banning of all but a few close mourners at funerals was particularly bitter, both for the mourners themselves and for those excluded. It made our lives seem even more unhinged and dream-like. When we served in Minnesota, burials of those who died in the winter were usually delayed until spring, unless the family objected. Some people felt extremely unsettled by not moving directly from the funeral to the burial, not finishing the journey to the grave; we did a lot of graveside services once the ground had thawed and burials began again. But during the pandemic, we lost the funeral service itself and that vital, grace-filled gathering of the community. We lost the whispered word, the touch of the hand, the tight embrace.

Most bitter of all had to be the deaths of the isolated: people dying alone, in hospitals or nursing homes, their loved ones not allowed to visit, sometimes not having seen them for weeks. The isolation took away the fundamental, creaturely vigil I spoke of at the beginning: the living being present and watching over the dying. Our endings were hidden from each other.

And yet, as I brooded on these things, it came to me that, once again, I was lamenting, with the voice of privilege, the loss of things which by no means were given to all. The world is now, and the world has always been, full of people who can't be with their dying loved ones, dying in wars, dying in refugee camps, dying in simple accidents far from home, dying in jail cells. Such deaths might come to anyone, making loss more bitter, though most of us can ignore the possibility most of the time. But, for example, military families must live with this fear as a fundamental condition of life. I heard a police officer's daughter say that, every time her father left the house, she feared she'd never see him again. African-American parents all say the same thing about their children.

And now I come to the revelations the pandemic brought about the malicious neglect, the racial inequities, and the enduring injustice of American society. From the start of the outbreak, the Trump administration's lack of preparation, its active scorn for competence, and its posturing leadership was only an extreme version of the Republican Party's approach to governing and the damage it inflicts on our social structures. As the virus spread, it traced America's moral fault lines. Minority populations, made vulnerable by decade upon decade of poor living and working conditions, contracted and died from COVID-19 at greater rates. Lack of health insurance and paid sick leave kept infected workers on the job, spreading the virus more broadly. Once employers started shutting down, it became glaring how little our country does to protect the unemployed. The American poor might as well have been in Defoe's London. Then, a couple of months into the outbreak, America's real plague erupted from the ugly depths of our life together.

A white police officer in Minneapolis arrested and was restraining George Floyd, an African-American man, by pressing his knee on Floyd's neck. Floyd was already handcuffed, lying face down on the street, while other officers helped restrain him. He had been accused of passing a counterfeit twenty-dollar bill. The officer kept his knee on Floyd's neck for eight minutes and forty-six seconds, a length of time that became notorious, until Floyd was dead. And, unlike the countless killings of African-Americans for several centuries by white authority figures, it was all recorded on video, seen around the world before the day was out. Floyd's death, though it was only the latest killing of an African-American by a white police officer, and not the first caught on video, ignited more protests than America had seen since the Vietnam War. Certainly, the cold-bloodedness of the killing drove the outrage; the officer, clearly in no danger himself, kept strangling Floyd as he begged for his life. No doubt the pent-up frustration and the economic threats brought by the virus gave their own energy to the outcries. The blind, ugly racism of white America, flaunted anew by more outrageous police conduct every few days, as well as by the racist rants and brutal orders of President Trump, seemed to merge with the virus into a powerful indictment of a nation that was destroying its own people.

It's not my purpose here to write a history of this time, nor to chronicle the failures and crimes of the United States. I want to raise up our racial conflicts, as I used Defoe's story, for another, different perspective on the pandemic.

Because of President Trump's own need to minimize the threat of the virus and his refusal to follow practices like social distancing and wearing face masks, the country was divided on the very measures we needed to curb the outbreak; though most supported them, the president's followers rejected and ridiculed them. So, when the protesters filled the streets, though most wore face masks, conservative commentators and the president's allies were quick to condemn the hypocrisy of liberals and progressives, risking infection by gathering in such large groups.

Here's my point: the instinct of the protesters was correct and came from an accurate assessment of the things that menace their lives and welfare. The screaming inequities of American life, rooted in racism so deep that white Americans are blind to it, really are a greater threat to them, both short and long term, than COVID-19. In fact, the virus has raged so terribly through minority communities precisely because of those inequities.

There are other threats as well. I ended my final chapter musing a bit on climate change and the blindness of people to its dangers. The coronavirus has almost entirely driven climate change from the news cycle. The virus, an immediate danger, with statistics that can rise spectacularly from day to day, is a headline grabbing phenomenon. Climate change, a slower threat, needn't be seen if you don't want to see it and you spend your time in air-conditioned offices and homes. But the world's ice is still melting, its temperatures and its seas are rising, its fires are greater, its storms more destructive, and the fossil-fuel companies, smiled on by the United States government, still scoff at calls to change.

As serious and as deadly as the virus itself is, it can still function, at the very same time, as an equally deadly distraction from other things quite capable of destroying us.

And those are my thoughts in this time of plague.

But what of my small, aging self? I'm still scribbling these thoughts on my bench under our gingko, now providing its summer shade for Yum-Yum and me. Has the virus brought my sure and certain death closer to me, or made it seem more sure and more certain? Has it made me brood more on it or feel its closeness?

Reading about what a serious case of the virus can do, and being, at seventy-four years of age, in one of the more vulnerable groups, I'm not at all eager to contract it and faithfully wear my masks, keep my distance, and mostly stay home. COVID-19 has joined the other diseases I fear I'm coming down with in the middle of the night, as I wake from nightmares coughing and gasping, but I can't say it's shifted or redefined my fears or my knowledge of frailty very much at all. I'm the same person I was at the end of the last chapter, aware of my luck in life, waiting for and wondering about and sometimes wishing for my departure, reasonably sure that the human race I know, the blind, the one-eyed, and the visionary, will continue its struggles without me.

www.ingramcontent.com/pod-product-compliance
Lightning Source LLC
Chambersburg PA
CBHW050827160426
43192CB00010B/1922